Mourning Journey

Choosing to Live
When Happily Ever After Dies

Lisa Schultz-Fred

Sacred Press Publishing

Mourning Journey

Choosing to Live When Happily Ever After Dies

Sacred Press Publishing, LLC

Editor: Madalyn Stone
Cover Design: Deana Riddle
Cover Photo: Kirsten Danielson/kdesignsphotography.com
Formatting: RikHall.com
ISBN 978-0-9970987-0-9
1 7 1 2 2 0 1 5

This book is dedicated to the dearest loves my heart has ever known.

To Jesus Christ, my Savior, and first love, you turned my mourning into joy. It is an honor for me to proclaim you and make you known through the words of this book.

To my beloved Patrick, where do I begin? You inspired me in life…and you continue to inspire me in death. After you died, I was ushered into a labor room of grief. I did not know what would be birthed out of my sorrow, but I was confident it would be beautiful. It took me nine months, Pat, to write this book. In addition to our children, you helped me birth another beautiful legacy. Forever there will be a place in my heart that will only belong to you. Until we meet again…

To Benjamin, Jenna and Jared, my treasured blessings. When you were little and I held you in my arms, I longed to keep you there, safe and protected from the harsh realities of life. Knowing that was not possible, my prayer was that you would grow in strength and character so when faced with the harsh realities, you would not be destroyed. You've had to walk a path you would have never chosen to travel and I'm in awe of how you've walked it in such grace and strength. You continue to bring honor to your dad in how you live. I'm crazy in love with each of you.

To Kevin, my cherished husband. Falling in love with me totally changed your world. You were willing to give up what was familiar in your life to become totally immersed in the unfamiliar of mine. I believe that when God made you, He was also thinking of me, knowing you would be the stitches that would mend the fabric of my broken heart. You have graciously allowed the memory of Pat to remain alive in the hearts of my children and me and for that I am forever grateful. The love between us is uniquely ours and I pray you will always feel secure knowing I fully belong to you.

To my adorable grandchildren, Nathalie, Lincoln, Noah, and Kaelyn and to those yet to be born: I look at each of you in total amazement. You have ushered me into a new realm of loving someone that I have never experienced before. There is no limit to the amount of joy you bring to my life. Papa Pat lives through each one of you and you are part of his legacy.

Contents

Foreword

I first saw Lisa at a "Living Free in Christ" conference that I was conducting in Minnesota. It was hard not to notice her, but natural beauty does not a whole person make, which she was in the process of discovering. In a worldly sense, and even in a Christian sense, she seemed to have it all. She was raised by loving Christian parents who were well respected. Being attractive, intelligent, and personable, she was popular. Life was good in rural Minnesota.

Then a crisis at home, turned their family dynamics upside down and Lisa committed a personal indiscretion that alienated friends, each negatively impacting her life. It only takes one pimple to threaten the appearance of a teenage girl. Then Satan added insult to injury by peppering her mind with insidious accusations. Lisa kept up appearances, as we all do, but her internal world was full of insecurities. Her once-happy life was now plagued by depression. The pinnacles of social status, performance, and appearance soon crumble under hostile rejection, self-condemnation, and the relentless pursuit of the accuser.

Lisa discovered who she was in Christ and found her freedom through genuine repentance and faith in God. She learned how to tear down mental strongholds and win the battle for her mind. She became one of our ministry associates and was helping others find their identity and freedom in Christ with the blessings of her committed Christian husband. This would be a fairly normal story of transition from our natural identity to our identity in Christ and from the insecurities of this fallen world to the security all believers have in Christ. However, tragedy struck, and her husband was killed while on a family bicycle outing. Lisa rode in the ambulance, but he never made it to the hospital alive. How does one survive when the world crumbles around you?

We live and make plans for tomorrow and the coming months as though life will go on normally. We assume that employment will continue as well as our health and the support structures of friends, family, and church. It is a relatively stress-free existence if you are living a righteous and responsible life, but what happens when confronted by a crisis or the loss of a spouse, child, home, or job? Such losses sow the seeds of depression. The first response is denial—a refusal to accept the crisis or loss. Facing the truth is too painful, and we consciously or subconsciously think it is a bad dream or a trick that someone is playing on us. Denial can last for seconds or many years, and some are permanently taken off course because they never deal with the reality of what they lost.

Anger is the next reaction when the thinking, "No, not me!" turns to "Why me?" Some will try to bargain with God or others to undo the loss, but when it can't be altered, they begin to struggle with feelings of helplessness and hopelessness. Any crisis allowed by God is never meant to destroy us but to reveal who we are. While the loss is permanent, it doesn't have to permanently affect us in a negative way. When reality sets in, we have the choice of resignation or restoration. *Resignation* is letting the circumstances of life dictate who we are and refusing to accept what cannot be changed. Choosing to resign from life leaves one depressed, bitter, and resentful.

Restoration is accepting the consequences of living in a fallen world and choosing to believe that we can grow through the crisis and come through it better people than we were before. A prolonged depression signifies an overattachment to people, places, and things that we have no right or ability to control. Helen Keller once said, "The bend in the road is not the end of the road unless you fail to make the turn."

Lisa made the turn. It wasn't easy being a single parent and sole provider of a family. It was a time of reassessing who she really was. Fortunately, she had already internalized her identity in Christ but even that gets deepened for those who bounce back from devastating losses. Lisa is a survivor. She could have sat around, licked her wounds, and felt sorry for herself. Instead, she chose to accept the challenges of life and put the needs of her children ahead of her own. Lisa is a shining example of Romans 5:3-5,

> "We rejoice in our sufferings, knowing that suffering produces endurance, and endurance produces character, and character produces hope, and hope does not disappoint, because God's love has been poured into our hearts through the Holy Spirit who has been given to us."

This is not a rags-to-riches story. It is the story of one woman's struggle to be all that God created her to be, and it has a very good ending.

Dr. Neil T. Anderson
Founder and President Emeritus of Freedom in Christ Ministries

Introduction

For over twenty-one years, I wrote love notes to my husband. This was by far the most difficult one I ever had to write…

Hi Hon,

Almost twenty-one years ago, you and I began our lifelong journey with the words, "To have and to hold, for better or worse, for richer or poorer, in sickness and health, ***till death do us part."*** *Thank you for being so faithful to the vows you spoke to me. I never once doubted how much you loved me. I'm going to miss your words of love that flowed from your mouth so easily and so often. The Bible says that the two become one flesh. You and I were one flesh and part of me is gone now but I'm looking to my Lord and Savior to fill up my emptiness. Thank you for giving me my most treasured possessions, our three children. I will always have a part of you because of them. My entire being longs for you. But I will not grieve like those who have no hope because my hope is in the Lord whom you and I served. The One who called you home on Saturday, will call me home one day and I will see you again, my precious husband. Until then, I will love our children and help them discover and fulfill their life dreams. I will speak of the rare love that God gave to you and me. And I will speak of the beauty that He will give me for the ashes of my grief. I will not say good-bye to you my best friend, because I'll see you later. I love you, Lisa*

The events of August 20, 2005 forever changed my life when a paramedic told me that my husband of twenty-one years did not make it. The path my family was walking was well illuminated that morning, but a few short hours later, there was penetrating darkness. My childhood dreams of "happily ever after" had abruptly ended.

***

It was a beautiful, sunny Saturday when my husband Pat and I and our thirteen year-old son, Jared were invited by friends to travel an hour and a half north to a town called Park Rapids, Minnesota. A former railroad bed had been tarred and was now a forty-nine-mile, multiple-use trail. Our plan was bike riding on the trail in the afternoon followed by dinner in a quaint little town along the trail before returning home that evening.

Twenty-five minutes into the ride, my husband and a truck converged at an intersecting country road. Neither could stop in time, and Pat crashed head on into the side of the pickup. I was farther back on the trail so I did not witness the accident but our son Jared did. What heartbreak awaited me as I approached the accident site to see my husband lying there, his body broken, and our precious son trying to comfort his father.

Forty-five agonizing minutes passed before Pat slipped away from this life into the arms of Jesus. The unthinkable happened. How would I break the news to my two children who were at home waiting for us to return? "Please God don't let this be true. Let me wake up and realize I've had a bad dream." But I could not even begin to wish away this nightmare.

As I was forced to live out a new reality in the days that followed, I had to draw on the supernatural strength of a God that loved me and had carried me through agonizing times in the past. I had to remind myself daily that He had always proved to be faithful to me and He would not fail me this time, either.

> *A Mourning Journey is about a life of preparation. Romans 5:3 says,*
>
> *"We also rejoice in our sufferings, because we know that suffering produces perseverance; perseverance, character; and character, hope. And hope does not disappoint us, because God has poured out His love into our hearts by the Holy Spirit, whom He has given us."*

My previous sufferings had produced in me perseverance, character, and hope. Many times in years past, I would cry out to God and ask, "Why Lord? Why am I in mental torment and anguish of soul? How long, oh Lord, will depression be my constant companion? How long will the enemy's taunt plague me?"

I didn't know it at the time, but His answer was, "Long enough to make you strong enough for what you will face in the future."

A Mourning Journey is about discovering my true, unchanging identity in Jesus. If my identity had been only Lisa, the wife of Pat Schultz, then who was I the day he died? I was Lisa, child of God, friend of Jesus, bride of Christ. Even when the circumstances of life changed the direction of my life, I knew who I was.

A Mourning Journey is about walking my children through the grief process and teaching them how to "suffer strong." It is so true that when your child hurts, you hurt. My pain was magnified as I tried to balance being strong for my children and still allowing myself to deeply grieve the loss of my soul mate.

A Mourning Journey is about finding the freedom to love again. When you've made a vow to love and be faithful to the one you marry, it's difficult to find, even in death, the permission to break that vow. God had in His perfect plan for me to meet and fall in love with a man named Kevin Fred. God knew that Kevin was the one who would not feel threatened by another man whom I would always love. Kevin was the one who held me on our wedding night as I cried one more time. Kevin was the one who unconditionally loved another man's children without trying to take the place of their father.

A Mourning Journey is about understanding the sovereignty of Almighty God in the midst of suffering.

If your happily ever after has also died, no matter what that might be, my prayer is that the pages of this book will inspire you to keep on living.

Chapter 1
Forever Changed

It was six days before Passover when Jesus arrived in the town of Bethany. He was invited to a dinner in which He was to be the guest of honor. Lazarus, whom Jesus had raised from the dead, was among those reclining at the table. While they reclined, Mary, the sister of Lazarus, came to Jesus holding an alabaster jar of expensive perfume. She broke the jar open and poured the perfume on Jesus's feet and proceeded to wipe his feet with her hair. (see John 12:1-3)

A broken woman with a broken jar of perfume spilled out at the feet of Jesus, and scripture tells us that those in the room were blessed by the fragrance that filled it. Such a contrast. How could "brokenness" be a blessing to others? I soon learned how after I lay broken at the feet of Jesus.

***

August 15th, 2005, began a week of intense emotions. It was a Monday; a day I had been dreading for eighteen years; we were packing up our first-born, Benjamin, and moving him to college. He was only going to be seventy-five miles away, but in my mind he might as well have been moving to another country because my baby was no longer going to be living in our home.

That morning, we backed our truck into the garage and carefully packed the things he needed. He was sharing an apartment with friends, so it wasn't just clothes: there was the coffee table that his grandparents had bought for him still in its original box; there were the freshly washed linens and comforter set that still smelled of the fabric softener and held the stains of his mother's tears; there was a box of odds and ends that I collected from our home that I was sure he needed in order to make his new apartment his home.

It was afternoon when my husband Pat, Ben, and I got in the truck to make that seventy-five-mile journey. I wanted Ben to be excited, and I wanted him to believe I was excited for him, but the lump in my throat would not go away, and the tears were always ready to spill over. I had to keep saying to myself, "get a grip."

It was early evening by the time the truck was unloaded and all his things were placed in the apartment. We were deciding where to eat when Pat got a call from his twin brother Mike; a storm had come through the resort that we owned together and had destroyed one of our cabins. We still had the remainder of the summer vacation season to get through with hunting season to follow, and now we were without a cabin that had been rented.

As we drove home, I could see how Pat was preoccupied with thoughts of the storm damage. I must say it also gave me something else to think about other than the son I had just left behind. When we got back to the resort, although it was dark, we were eager to see what other harm the winds had caused. As the headlights from our truck shone in front of us, they revealed a lot of downed branches, disheveled docks and boats, and a badly beaten up Northern cabin.

The next morning, Pat went to work, and between cleaning up downed tree branches and straightening crooked docks, he spent time on the computer looking for building plans for a new cabin. Both he and Mike had many skills, including carpentry, so he knew they had a big project ahead of them. After a long and tiring day of work, he came home to me – a blubbering mess. One of my chicks had left the nest, and I was mourning the change.

For some reason, I remember Wednesday night of that week in particular. We were lying in bed, and I was crying once again. Pat tenderly took me in his arms and allowed me to cry it out. I can't say that he totally understood how I was feeling. He loved Ben as much as I did, but he was able to think more logically: Ben isn't far from home. He will be back on weekends to work at the resort. We can go take him out for a meal at any time.

Yes, but I still had to look at his empty room. I had to deal with the deafening silence when I didn't hear his familiar voice saying, "Mom, where is my ...?" I'm so thankful Pat was patient with my roller-coaster emotions.

By Friday, I was handling things better. My boy was on his way home for the weekend. In the midst of all that was going on at the resort, Pat was also helping with a remodeling project at church. Like I said, he had many talents, and the one he was using at church was laying a ceramic tile floor. He went to work at the church that Friday afternoon and worked into the early evening.

I was busy at home washing and packing a few more things for Ben that he had not taken on Monday. I had fed the family, and Pat's supper was warming in the oven. The Minnesota Vikings were playing a preseason game that night, and I knew Pat would need some down time when he got home. Eating a hot meal while watching the game was a perfect way for him to unwind, and that is exactly what he did.

Early that evening, the phone rang. It was my friend Cindy asking if we were interested in going bike riding the next day in Park Rapids, Minnesota. Tim and Cindy had been our dear friends for many years, and they had a son the same age as our youngest son, Jared, so the six of us would be going on this adventure together. Pat was in favor of the idea, but he wanted to finish the tiling job at the church in the morning first, so we planned to meet at noon at Tim and Cindy's home.

Saturday could not have been more beautiful. The sun was shining brightly. It was not too hot or too humid, which is rare for the end of August. Pat got up early and went to the church as planned. By the time he got home, we were running late, so he was in a hurry to shower. Our daughter, Jenna, was using our bathroom to get ready for the day, and when her dad said she needed to be done so he could get in, there were a few tense moments between them. How painful that memory became for my precious girl in just a few short hours.

With our bikes securely tied down in the back of the truck, Pat, Jared, and I climbed into the cab and we were off. Tim and Cindy had a bike rack attached to the back of their van that fit all six of our bikes, making it convenient to take one vehicle to our destination.

Nestled in the heart of Minnesota lakes country is a fifty-mile trail connecting several small communities. Towering over this paved railroad bed are white pine, spruce fir, and hardwood trees that offer shade from the penetrating sun. If you are careful to pay attention, you just might see a raccoon, a red fox, a whitetail deer, a beaver, or a porcupine.

Because the paved path was a railroad bed at one time, it is fairly level and smooth, which was wonderful for a novice biker like me. I could multitask while I rode— meaning pedal, talk without being short of breath, and even watch for wildlife. That level path also took us through quaint little towns with fun restaurants, so our plan was to make one of those restaurants our final stop that day.

In the hour-and-a-half van ride, we shared a lot of laughs. The two young boys had a fill-in-the-blank storybook. They were busy asking us to give them words such as adjectives, nouns, verbs, and so on, which they wrote in the blank space. After each line was filled in, they would read back to us the crazy story we had just created with the added words. It was so much fun to hear the boys laughing and joining in with them. I needed that after a week of crying.

I did notice how Pat sat in the front passenger seat, deep in thought. He did not really get into the silliness with the rest of us. After being married to this man for almost twenty-one years, I knew that he was preoccupied with the events of the past week, in particular, the cabin that had to be replaced. I was happy that he was able to get away from it all, even for just an afternoon. I knew the summer air, the exercise, and the beauty of God's creation would refresh him.

I shamefully confess that Pat and I always required our children to wear bike helmets, but we did not practice that same discipline. However, when we were getting ready to start our ride, Tim said they had an extra helmet and offered it to Pat and me. I was shocked when Pat said he'd wear it. He was a daredevil and always had a sense of invincibility about him, so I never thought he wanted to feel hindered by a helmet.

Since we did not plan on returning to the original spot of our departure, Cindy drove ahead with the van to park in the little town of Dorsette where we were going to have dinner that night. We would meet up with her there, bike farther down the trail, and then return to Dorsette. As Cindy drove away, the remaining five of us started down the path.

The two thirteen-year-old boys were not about to waste any time; a leisurely ride was not part of their plan that day. The trail was wide enough for Tim, Pat, and me to ride side by side as long as we did not meet anyone else on the path, which is how we started out. But the adventurous spirit of a young boy still captivated my husband's heart, so he chose to speed ahead to ride with the two thirteen-year-olds. I vividly remember as he got several yards ahead, he turned back to look at us. In his mind, the race was on. He wanted to beat Tim and me to Dorsette and needed to calculate his lead. I did not know that was the last time I would see his body whole and strong.

Tim and I continued on our leisurely pace. About fifteen minutes after that final glance from Pat, Peter—Tim and Cindy's son—came frantically riding back toward us to say Pat had run into the side of a pickup. Tim set out at a record pace while giving Peter instructions to bike next to me. Immediately, I felt my strength leave me, and I do not know how I continued to peddle.

My body trembled from head to toe. Fear and nausea set in at the thought of what I might possibly see when I arrived at the accident site. Life went into slow motion. I remember nothing about the ride from the place where Peter told us of the accident to the actual accident site.

As I approached that dreadful intersection, I saw several people standing around. I immediately looked for Pat. I held that same belief of his invincibility. His bike was lying there next to the pickup. Where was he? I was then drawn to a sound that I will never forget, my precious husband fighting for every breath. I turned my head in the direction of the sound, and there he lay along the side of the intersecting gravel road. Tim was with him, attempting to keep him calm.

My initial response was not to run to Pat to see what I could do to help but rather to flee and distance myself from his trauma. I could not bear seeing my husband suffer, and I knew Tim was there with him. I walked back several hundred feet on the bike path and took out my cell phone and called his brother Mike. Why that was my first reaction, I do not know.

When Mike answered the phone, I had to break the horrible news that went something like this: "Mike, Pat has had a terrible accident. A truck has hit him while we were biking. (I was not yet aware of the full details of what actually happened.) He is hurt really bad. It doesn't look good."

"No… No… No." I will never forget the tone of Mike's voice nor the anguish expressed in that one word repeated over and over. That is all I remember of our conversation.

Jared made his way over to me. I had not yet begun to comprehend what my baby boy had just experienced, being an eyewitness to the accident and then having to sit with his badly broken father until we got there. It was not me at that moment who comforted my son; it was he who comforted me when he put his arms around me and said, "The Lord is our strength, Mom. Let's pray, Mom."

I so needed a sanctuary at that moment, a place where I could feel safe and cared for. Jesus was our sanctuary, and Jared ushered me into the holy place of God's presence. I do not know how Jared and I formed our words that we cried out to God on the bike path that day, but I do know they included, "Help us. Heal him. Please God, please." I also know that other bikers who passed by saw a mother and son crying out to the One who was able to deliver them as they began a journey through the valley of the shadow of death.

After we prayed, I sat stunned, trying to wrap my mind around what was happening. A highway patrol officer came and knelt down beside me. I remember nothing of the conversation other than my asking him, "Should I be with him?"

For many, this question may seem strange. You may ask, "Why wouldn't you want to be with him?" My fight or flight response goes into flight mode in a traumatic situation. I want to flee and do what I can from a distance while others tend to the immediate need. But I knew by the officer's response, "Yes, I think you should," that I had to fight against my conditioned response.

"Jesus, you are my strength. I can do this. I can be who my husband needs me to be." I made my way over to Pat, and I knelt down over him and said, "Honey, I'm here." His eyes opened and met mine, and the look of terror displayed in those beautiful green eyes deeply penetrated my soul. Then they closed again as he continued fighting for every breath.

The ambulance finally arrived, so I needed to leave Pat's side so they could attend to him. One of the paramedics invited me to ride along in the ambulance. I quickly climbed into the passenger seat, eagerly wanting to get my husband the help he needed. Finally Pat was secure in the back, and we were ready to go with lights flashing and sirens sounding, warning other vehicles to get out of our way.

The driver handed me a clipboard with paperwork for me to fill out. Are you kidding me?! Please tell me how I can even remember something as familiar as Pat's birth date when all my mind can focus on are his words, "I can't breathe." At that moment, who cares whether or not we have insurance. I don't care what it costs, just don't let him die.

While I was trying to fill out the paperwork, the driver was talking to me. She told me we were going to the Park Rapids airport where a helicopter was meeting us to fly Pat to North Memorial Trauma Center in Minneapolis, Minnesota. I knew Pat was badly hurt, but to hear that a helicopter was meeting us brought home the reality of just how critical he was.

I made an attempt to encourage Pat to relax and breathe deeply not fully knowing that was not even possible. I was trapped in this vehicle. I could not escape the trauma that was occurring right behind me and being one flesh with the person suffering caused a suffering within me that was almost unbearable. That labored gasping for breath continued until we pulled into the airport, when suddenly there was nothing but silence. I realized at that moment that all silences are not equal. This one was quieter than all others. The paramedic attending him broke the silence when she cried out, "Pat! Pat!" I knew she was trying to call him back.

At that moment, the thought hit me, My husband is dying. All of a sudden it felt as if all of the air had been sucked out of the ambulance. Now I was the one laboring to breathe; I was being suffocated by fear and panic. As the ambulance came to a stop on the tarmac of the airport, I could not open the door fast enough. My conditioned response to flee had kicked in once again, but I did not make it far.

Opening the door, I fell to the ground. My initial thought was, "I'm going to lose all soundness of mind." I did not know if I was going to pass out or throw up from the trauma I was experiencing. I was stuck between the two worlds of reality and denial. Thankfully, the faces of my three precious children came to the forefront of my thoughts and the fight response kicked in. My choice at that moment was to continue to live for them, and the only way I knew how to do that was in the strength of Jesus. As I lay on the ground, broken, with my tears spilling out at the feet of Jesus, I proclaimed out loud the words of Job, "The Lord gave and the Lord has taken away. Blessed be the name of the Lord" (Job 1:20-21 NKJV).

Somehow, I was able to pick myself up off the ground and make my way to a chain-linked fence where I sat resting my back against it, trying to make sense of what was real. Tim, Cindy, Jared, and Peter had made their way to the airport and joined me as we waited to hear what was happening in the ambulance. The helicopter had arrived, and the roar of the blades was a constant reminder of my present reality. But what was taking them so long? Why are they not getting Pat transferred to the helicopter?

We waited and waited for what seemed to be an eternity. Finally, one of the paramedics approached us to say that Pat had gone into cardiac arrest and they were working on him. It was in those moments that he and I were simultaneously entering into two very opposite yet very real existences. While the man I loved was being ushered into the most brilliant light he had ever experienced, my world was getting darker. While his ears were hearing the most amazing praises being sung to his Savior, my ears were filled with a deafening silence as the helicopter blades were turned off, signifying to me that he was gone. The paramedics approached us once again. Their walk was slow and steady. There were no smiles on their faces; in fact, there were no expressions at all.

When our eyes met, all they could say was, "We are sorry. He did not make it." They asked if I wanted to go to the ambulance to see him.

I said, "No. He is not there. His body is, but he is with Jesus."

How do I explain such an answer? You might be thinking, "Weren't you crying hysterically or screaming at God, how can you do this to me?" The life I had known just one hour earlier was forever changed, so how could I say, seemingly nonchalantly, "He's not there, he is with Jesus?" My only answer is that I made a choice at that moment to believe God was sovereign and He was with me. The Bible talks about a peace that goes beyond our understanding, and that is what I experienced at that moment. I don't know why I was given this gift of a supernatural peace when others find it difficult to hold it together in the midst of tragedy. What I do know is the previous events of my life had been preparing me for this day.

Chapter 2
Innocence Lost

I think we can all be thankful that we don't know how this journey we call life will unfold. I once read,

> *"The path we are walking on is filled with twists and turns and hills that sometimes get in the way of our being able to see what lies ahead. The earth is a minefield with unseen enemies that lurk in unexpected places. Simply put, life can be scary here."*

Scary? As a young child, I would have said, "Are you kidding me? Life is great! "

The only fear I was battling against was from my older, identical twin sisters who told me that if anyone broke into our house, the intruder would "get me first" since my bedroom was the first one in our hallway.

Every night, I begged one of them to sleep in my room and let me sleep with the other twin, and every night it was the same answer, "No. Stay in your own bed."

So, as soon as I knew they were asleep, I sneaked into their room, untucked the covers at the foot of their bed, and slid in feet first. It was only right that my feet would be in their faces! All fear was gone when morning dawned, and I was ready for a new day.

I was blessed to be raised in a home where I was deeply loved by my parents. Attending Sunday school and church was part of our weekly routine. On Wednesdays, I was released from school after lunch to go to church for midweek instruction, and vacation Bible school was always a part of my summer schedule.

At a very young age, Jesus stole my heart. I don't remember when I first loved Him or when I first came to the realization of how much He loved me. I don't remember kneeling at an altar or beside my bed inviting Him to be the Lord of my life, but as long as I can remember, I always believed in my heart and always uttered in confession that Jesus is my Lord.

When I was about nine, my mom took a picture of me reading devotions to my stuffed animals and my beloved Mrs. Beasley doll. I guess I thought they needed saving, too. I also took every opportunity possible to share the love of Jesus with friends and family whether it was in a written note or talking about Him during sleepovers. My deep cry at birth not only started my physical life, it began my journey with Jesus. "Yet you brought me out of the womb; you made me trust in you, even at my mother's breast. From birth I was cast on you; from my mother's womb you have been my God" (Psalm 22:9-10).

I grew up in a neighborhood where there was no shortage of kids to play with. My summer days, before age ten, went something like this: I would wake to the sound of a morning dove cooing outside my window. I wouldn't hop out of bed quickly because I had to mentally plan my day. First I would get some chalk and make a hopscotch board on the sidewalk in front of our house. It was a perfect sidewalk for hopscotch. Each cement square was the ideal size to draw an *X* pattern from corner to corner. It took four squares and four *X*s and numbers one to twelve to complete the board. Then I had to find the perfect round stone— one that would roll straight to each number I wanted it to rest on. I often started the game alone, but it wasn't long until friends in the neighborhood joined me.

When we tired of hopscotch, we moved on to playing house. My grandfather built us a playhouse in our backyard. It was cute with a pitched roof and large windows but small in comparison to my friend's playhouse across the street. Mine was fine if I was playing alone, but I was thrilled when I was invited to Tara's. I would pack up my dolls, put on my play high heels, and strut across the street.

Our moms gave us their empty food containers that we used in our make-believe world of cooking. Our cupboards were filled with cereal boxes and rinsed-out soup cans. Freshly washed milk cartons filled our play refrigerator. I especially loved getting the tin cans that held Schilling spices. I could still smell what was once in them, giving a greater sense of reality to my make-believe world.

Bike riding was another favorite summer activity. I will never forget getting my first banana seat. It was almost as exciting as a bicycle built for two since both a friend and I had room on this seat to ride together. There were no wearing helmets back then. I got the full force of the breeze blowing through my thin blonde hair, and of course the faster I went, the better.

I always enjoyed getting a quarter from mom and riding my bike to a family-owned neighborhood market. We were fortunate to have two within three blocks of our home. On the days I had a quarter to spend, I chose the one that had the best penny candy, knowing I would have a little brown bag of sweetness clutched in my hand when I returned home.

When evening came, the neighborhood boys joined us girls in a friendly game of kick the can. It was a combination of tag, hide-and-seek, and capture the flag. I remember one time being a little too aggressive in kicking the can and breaking our basement window. That made for an exciting evening because a cat crawled through the broken glass and walked across the keys on our piano after we had gone to bed. If my memory serves me right, that cat was the catalyst for my confession.

As a child, it wasn't hard to say good-bye to summer because winter also brought an endless choice of fun things to do. We had a sledding hill just a couple blocks away from our home. I remember thinking "this hill is *huge*" and wondering if it would ever end as I slid down it. Today when I look at that same hill, I smile and think it is all about perspective, because it's not really huge at all.

Within walking distance from my home was Lake Alice. In the winter, an area on one end of the lake was cleared for ice skating. My friends and I would tie the laces of our skates together and hang them around our necks and make our way to the rink.

Evening was our favorite time to skate. The lights illuminated the rink, and the speaker on the warming house projected the popular songs of the 70s. When our fingers and toes were nearly frozen, the heat of the warming house beckoned us inside. I can still hear my skates clunking on the old wooden floor as I walked toward the warm stove. I stood there with my hands extended just enough to feel the warmth from the stove but not too close to be burned.

Snowmobiling with my dad was another highlight of winter. I loved hearing the roar of the engine and the smell of the fumes as a thick haze filled the garage, because I knew within moments we would be riding open trails.

I typically sat behind my dad holding on tight around his waist, but there were also times that he was brave enough to let me drive. Had he known the damage I would later do to our snowmobiles, I don't think he would ever have allowed me to take control of the handlebars. The day did come, however, when I was old enough to handle the snowmobile alone.

Starting the sled was always a challenge for me. One evening, Mom asked me to go to one of our neighborhood markets for milk. I was excited to take the snowmobile. On this particular night the sled was parked outside, facing the garage. I stood alongside that machine and pulled on the cord with all my might. When the engine started to engage, I put my thumb on the throttle to give it a little gas. A little? Hardly. The next thing I knew, I was lying flat on my back in the middle of the driveway as the snowmobile lunged forward hitting the house.

My dear mom came outside and stood over me as I lay on the ground and said, “Lisa, what are you doing?”

I felt like saying it was a nice night to look up at the stars, but I was too taken aback that she didn’t ask if I was OK. I wish I could say that was the only time that happened, but unfortunately, that is not the case. The next time, it was in the afternoon. Similar scenario, with me starting the snowmobile while it was parked outside facing the garage. Once again, I throttled too aggressively while starting it, but this time I did not let go of the handlebars. A girlfriend of mine was there to witness me being dragged alongside a runaway snowmobile. With a hard right turn, my legs flew in the air as the sled did a sharp 180 and made an abrupt stop as it hit the inside garage wall. My thought as I looked at the once horizontal ski that was now vertical was, “What would I tell dad this time?”

Of course, included in those wonderful childhood days were school days. I have some of the sweetest kindergarten memories. Part of our morning routine was placing our tiny rugs on the floor to take a rest. Mine was a multicolored, braided rug. At the end of the quiet time, my teacher decided who was the "best rester." There was an elf that sat on her desk that she used to rub the cheek of the "best rester." The chosen child then got to take the elf and "wake up" the other children by rubbing their cheeks with the elf's raised hand. I loved when I was chosen.

At Christmastime, we made a special gift for our mothers. Mom picked up whole cloves (in a wonderful, Schilling tin) for me, and I took those along with an orange to school. With every ounce of love, I carefully pushed a clove through the skin of the orange until the entire surface was covered. The smell was amazing, and I was excited for that scent to be a part of mom's kitchen. Even today, I still find myself pulling cloves from my spice cabinet, opening the cover, and breathing in the scent deeply. Immediately, my memory takes me back to a sweet time long ago.

In second grade, I was transferred to a grade school closer to our home. Built in 1905, Lincoln Elementary was far from up to date, but it exuded warmth and character. There were three entrances, and whichever one you stepped into, you were greeted by a massive, wooden staircase with beautifully ornate banisters. Each stair creaked with every step taken, and the sound of our shoes on the wooden floors echoed through the high ceilings.

We didn't have lockers, but we did have cloak halls attached to each classroom, complete with black iron hooks to hang our book bags and jackets on. In the winter, it made for quite a smelly classroom as our wet outerwear filled that cloak hall. But that was just fine. It was a reminder for the afternoon of how much fun we had experienced at recess.

Even after I left this elementary school, there was something about it that drew me back each year to visit. Was it those creaky wooden floors and high ceilings? Was it the familiar smells of the lunchroom and stinky cloak halls? Was it the teachers who not only took an interest in your education but also in you as a person? It was all of those things. Every year until I graduated from high school, I went back for a dose of nostalgia that I never tired of.

The final year Lincoln Elementary was open was 1981. The local paper came to take a picture of the last student body to attend this historic building. Guess who got in the picture? You got it! There I stood in the back row with the teachers. It was my annual pilgrimage day. I felt both silly and honored at the same time to be in the photo.

It was my freshman year in college when my mom called me and said, "Guess what they started doing today? Demolishing Lincoln Elementary." I started to cry. It was in those tears that I truly realized what an impact the school had made on my life during those formative years. It had been a place of stability when things were shaky at home.

Mom was so surprised by my response that she graciously tried to soften the blow by saying, "Well, they saved the banisters." She even went and got me an exterior brick so that I could have a piece of history—and a piece of my childhood— to hang onto.

I wish I could say that the picture I've just painted of my early childhood years remained in bright and cheerful colors. However, that was not the case. What I read is true—the path of life is filled with twists and turns but also stones, cracks, and ruts, and each one of these alters the course of our journey.

In the midst of my joy-filled days in grade school, my older sister was in the depths of a crisis. At fourteen, she found herself looking for love in all the wrong places, and in an attempt to find self-worth and unconditional love she became pregnant at that very young age.

During a time when I was listening to a story about a spider that was creating words in a web in order to save a pig from certain death, a new life was being created in the womb of my sister. At nine years old, I had so many questions. Why is Dad so angry? Why is mom crying? Why is my sister's stomach getting bigger? How did that baby get in there?! I was learning about pigs and spiders, not the birds and the bees.

It was a cool November day in 1972 when my sister gave birth to a baby girl. The baby was placed in the arms of a husband and wife who were unable to conceive, and this precious little girl would call them mom and dad. My sister named her Nadine, and for many years, that was the name I used as I prayed for this girl I had never met.

Several months later, my sister became pregnant with her second child. I have a vivid picture of the day we found out she was having another baby. Our pastor had come over, and we were in the kitchen when my dad got home from work. As the news of her pregnancy was shared with dad, he took the briefcase in his hand and threw it against the kitchen wall. I was terrified by the display of my father's anger. My childlike mind could not fully comprehend what was taking place.

The decision was made that she would keep this baby, and midway through the pregnancy, she married the baby's father. He enlisted in the Navy shortly after Paul was born, so the three of them moved to San Diego, California, where he was stationed. Before they left, my mom took the sleeper baby Paul had worn the night before their departure and placed it in her drawer. On many days, she removed it from her dresser, held it up to her nose, inhaled deeply, and cried. Her baby had had a baby—her grandson—and many miles were separating them.

In so many aspects, my sister was still a child herself, but she took on the role of being a mother with much love and maturity. Being so far away from home, she did not have the physical support of her family, but she loved and cared for that baby boy as if she had performed the task many times before.

She also faced stresses in her marriage that no woman, no matter what age, should ever have to endure. Physical, mental, and emotional abuses were daily threats in her life. When she made the choice to leave California and a life of fear, mom and dad got her on a flight back home. Tucked away in my mind is a picture of her frail frame walking toward us as she got off the plane, but the baby in her arms had a smile from ear to ear. He was secure in his mother's love.

Society can be cruel in their judgment of perceived failures in others. We all hold secrets that we pray no one will ever find out. If there are no visual signs of what we have done, we get the convenience of working it out alone or with a trusted friend or counselor. My sister did not have this option. The choices she made were there for a whole community to see and believe me, the responses were not always kind. There is a familiar phrase that says, "Sticks and stones may break my bones, but words will never hurt me." That could not be further from the truth. Words cut like a knife, leaving a wound open and raw for a long time, and even after the wound heals, there is still a scar.

I went several years feeling relatively unscathed by my sister's pregnancies. I was able to separate what was happening with her and still be a young girl enjoying life. That all changed when I started dating and experienced the first wounding words spoken directly to me. I remember being at a friend's house when a boyfriend called to tell me he was not allowed to date me.

His father had said to him, "You know what those Ferber girls are like."

I felt the knife going in. It wasn't a clean cut, and the pain was excruciating.

As a result of those words, and without even realizing it, a lie was starting to form in my mind. It was saying to me that "I wasn't good enough. I didn't measure up to the other girls."

After my sister's pregnancies, I was terrified of speaking to my parents about having a boyfriend. I was fearful that they thought that I would get pregnant. In my efforts to protect them, I didn't tell my mom and dad about any time I spent with a boyfriend. I remember specifically in junior high, walking home after a football game with my first heartthrob, but telling my parents I was walking home with one of my girlfriends.

As the Bible confirms, "Be sure your sins will find you out," and mine did. The girl I said I was walking home with called my house looking for me. My dad immediately set out to find me. I made it home before him, and I can still hear his car pull into the driveway and the force he used to put the shift into park. My attempt to protect my parents was perceived as rebellion and my backside received the brunt of my dad's anger.

To compensate for the fear of disappointing my parents and other authority figures, I set out to succeed and make a name for myself that would make the people in my life proud. I thought, "My identity will be in my accomplishments, and my security will be in my popularity." As long as I was well liked and popular with my peers, life was good, but the end of the good life was peering over the horizon at the start of my junior year in high school.

I was excited to be back at school after summer vacation and hanging out with friends I had spent little time with over the summer. The fall was always my favorite time of year. I loved the changing colors, the warm days, and the cool, crisp nights. I loved Friday night football games cheering on the Fergus Falls Otters. I loved homecoming week—the skits, coronation, powder-puff football, and the homecoming dance.

The year started out like previous ones with a lot of excitement and anticipation for what the year would bring. As junior class president, I was in charge of the junior/senior prom, and I was ready to meet that challenge with the planning and fund-raising that was a part of this school year. I did not anticipate the twists and turns and hills that were lying on the path ahead and were going to alter the course of my life forever.

My relationship with Jesus did not keep me from making poor choices. In the fall of that year, my parents and I went to visit family in Minneapolis. I ended up going to the home of my cousin's friend. We were sitting around the kitchen table drinking beer, thinking we were so mature. Another friend came over with a pipe and marijuana. Feeling invincible, I put it up to my mouth while it was being passed around—and yes, Mr. Clinton, I inhaled. The following moments were some of the scariest of my life. Some might consider this an exhilarating high, but I was terrified by the way I felt.

All I remember is the room spinning, and all I wanted was to feel "normal." I ran outside where my cousin and his friends followed, and I knelt down in the front of the car crying out to Jesus to help me. Now I terrified everyone else! I begged my cousin to take me back to his home because I knew my Bible was there, and I longed to have it in my hands. I clutched it tightly to my chest while I slept that night, and before falling asleep, I promised God not to do that again if He would just help me through the night.

That experience introduced a fear into my life of not being in control. I had already experimented with alcohol and knew the feeling of being drunk, but now the thought of any substance altering my state of mind terrified me. I believe it was God's intervention, protecting me from the addictive nature that plagues many of my family members.

I did a lot of soul-searching in the car on the way home that weekend. I hated the choice I had made to smoke the pot. I determined I never wanted to feel that way again and resolved to make better decisions that were God honoring and more responsible. The conviction of my sin and the realization that I had disappointed the Lord was excruciating for me.

My junior year was also a very trying time with relationships. Throughout my school years, I never lacked for friends. I was well liked and well respected, but once again, I did not use good judgment, and I devastated a dear friend. At a time when she needed the love and support of her best friend, I added salt to the festering wounds in her life by causing a breakup between her and her boyfriend. This not only destroyed my relationship with her, but I also lost the respect and acceptance of other friends.

I now observed friendship from a distance. I hated going to school and watching groups of friends gathering in the halls, in the lunchroom, laughing at their lockers, and making plans. I did not feel like I belonged anywhere. Rarely, if ever, did I receive a phone call inviting me to do something. The silence penetrated deep into my soul, and it did not take long for depression to set in.

Depression is one of the most painful experiences of the human soul. It robs you of life itself by sucking joy, peace, and contentment out of your very being. It follows you like a shadow, and even when you are around others, it does not loosen its grip. It is defined as "a mood disorder in which feelings of sadness, loss, anger, or frustration interfere with everyday life for an extended period of time." [1]

Loss. That word alone is painful. It was the loss of friendships that ushered me into a season of deep loneliness. I wasn't completely alone, however. Tormenting thoughts were my constant companion. There was no end to the voices in my mind telling me, I'm worthless. I'm a horrible friend. Nobody likes me. God has abandoned me. Things will never change. No matter how hard I tried, I could not get rid of these unwanted intruders.

The taunting thoughts were relentless during the day, and I was so relieved to fall asleep at night only to be awakened in sheer panic and fear that those thoughts were true of me. I lay in bed, eyes wide open, heart racing, palms sweating, and crying out to God, "What is this life all about? Why am I here? Am I losing my mind?" I really wondered if I had a serious, incurable mental illness that required me to be institutionalized for the rest of my life.

In Psalm 13:2, David asks a question of God, "How long must I wrestle with my thoughts and every day have sorrow in my heart?" I never enjoyed watching a wrestling match where two people struggled to maneuver out of awkward holds, yet I found myself in a wrestling match of sorts—a wrestling match for control of my soul. The Psalmist David had said it perfectly.

My opponent—tormenting, self-destructive thoughts—had me stubbornly pinned, and I had to cry out like David did in the next verse, "Come quickly to help me oh Lord my

God. Look on me and answer me…give light to my eyes, or I will sleep in death." I was not suicidal, but if God had divinely chosen to take me to heaven, I would have been okay with that.

A bed partner of depression is hopelessness. The American sociologist Lewis Mumford wrote in *The Conduct of Life* (1951), "A man can live three weeks without food, three days without water, and three minutes without air, but he cannot live three seconds without hope." I don't think there is a more terrifying feeling than hopelessness. When you are in the midst of it, you search for hope like a hidden treasure. Many times, like this following poem so beautifully illustrates, we draw on the hope of others until ours is restored.

Borrowed Hope

Lend me your hope for a while,
I seem to have mislaid mine.
Lost and hopeless feelings accompany me daily.
Pain and confusion are my companions.
I know not where to turn.
Looking ahead to the future times
Does not bring forth images of renewed hope.
I see mirthless times, pain-filled days, and more tragedy.
Lend me your hope for awhile,
I seem to have mislaid mine.
Hold my hand and hug me,
Listen to all my ramblings.
I need to unleash the pain and let it tumble out.
Recovery seems so far and distant,
The road to healing, a long and lonely one.
Stand by me. Offer me your presence,

Your ears and your love.
Acknowledge my pain, it is so real and ever present.
I am overwhelmed with sad and conflicting thoughts.
Lend me your hope for awhile.
A time will come when I will heal,
And I will lend my renewed hope to others.

Eloise Cole, Scottsdale, AZ (1942-2005)

What is hope? It is the present assurance of some future good. It is holding on to the belief that things will get better. It is to desire something with confident expectation of its fulfillment. I had a measure of hope within me that kept me going, but as the days of sadness turned into weeks of depression, I knew I needed help to hold onto the fleeting measure of hope that I was clinging to.

In high school, I was trained as a teenage health consultant, which basically meant that when fellow classmates were struggling with issues in life, I knew the resources available in our community to help them. Now, it was my turn to look to those resources. My self-confident, independent nature was not carrying me through this season of darkness, and I made an appointment at a local counseling center to meet with a Christian counselor.

I don't recall how many times we met or even what we talked about in our sessions, but I do very vividly remember walking out of the building one day and noticing the sun was shining. It wasn't that the sun had not been shining in the preceding days. It just had not been able to penetrate my darkness.

I heard the birds singing and felt the breeze against my face, and all of it was refreshing. It felt as though it were the first time I had experienced life. My depression had lifted—the symptoms of my depression, that is. Lying dormant in my subconscious mind were lies I believed about myself—that I was unlovable, unacceptable, and unworthy—and it was not long before I sought to have my identity needs met in my prince charming.

Chapter 3
Lost Inside of Love

In the summer of 1981, the only path I wanted to be on was a fifteen-mile stretch of paved roads that led me to a family-owned fishing resort on Ten Mile Lake. I knew behind the counter in the campground office was a handsome young man I had my eyes on. I was nineteen at the time and he was twenty-one.

It is hard to find anything more beautiful than a Minnesota lake in the summertime, and Ten Mile Lake was no exception. Nestled between two lakes, North and South Ten Mile, was a family fishing resort that was purchased in 1906 by Anthony and Anna Prohosky. They continued to run the resort until their daughter Nellie and her husband Fred Schultz took it over. Fred and Nell gave birth to two sons, Jerry and Bob. They were the third generation to own and operate the resort.

In 1962, Jerry and Bob decided to go out on a limb and build a steakhouse on the property. Up until that point, they served burgers and beer out of a small stand across the road from the lake. Seeing the need for a good steakhouse/dinner club not only for the vacationers but also for the locals, they built the steakhouse. It quickly became well known for the quality of food and atmosphere.

It was a treasured destination for many families who continued to make an annual pilgrimage to the resort each summer. Twelve cabins of varying sizes were located on the property, each with a lakeside view. At the end of summer vacation, families often rebooked the same cabin for the following summer. It was their home away from home for whatever time they spent there.

The campground had sites for over ninety campers. In the earlier years, overnight and weekend guests occupied most of the sites, but as time passed, they became seasonal rentals for the summer months. For several summers, my parents rented a campsite for the month of July until they, too, secured a seasonal site. It was definitely a favorite vacation spot for both my immediate and extended family.

It was actually the summer of 1979 that I first locked eyes with Pat Schultz. I was sitting around the campfire with several family members when he came walking through our campsite with a fishing pole and tackle box in hand. Wow! Was he ever handsome—thick dark hair, penetrating green eyes, and a smile that could light up a room. My aunt, a seasonal resident at the resort, knew Pat well and struck up a conversation with him. While they talked, I made mention of his good looks to my uncles as we sat around the fire. Big mistake. My uncles were notorious for mercilessly teasing, and Pat was definitely within earshot to hear their taunts. I felt heat rising from my feet all the way to the top of my head. Being blonde and fair skinned, I was unable to hide my embarrassment. As much pleasure as it gave me to look at him, I was relieved when he continued on to make his big catch.

Aunt Elaine knew the fish she wanted Pat to hook that night, and I was it. After sitting by the fire for a while, she invited me to walk with her out to the point, a popular spot on the resort for shore fishing, to see if Pat was having any success. I quickly put aside the embarrassment I had felt minutes before, and we walked the rugged path along the water's edge to where Pat was sitting on a large rock with his line in the water.

I honestly cannot remember if he had any fish on his stringer, but I do remember how my aunt conveniently excused herself while encouraging me to stay and keep Pat company. I graciously accepted and found another large rock where I could watch him fish and hope for words to fill any awkward silence, but to my relief, that wasn't a problem.

It could not have been a more beautiful setting for the beginning of a romance. It was a warm summer evening with a full moon reflecting off the calm water. We stayed on the point talking long after Pat caught his last fish. I was secretly hoping that I was Pat's greatest catch that night.

As we walked back to my camper, and I watched him go inside his home conveniently located next to our campsite, I knew I was going to have a hard time falling asleep that night. Like Bambi and the rest of the animals in that animated movie, I was "twitter-pated."

Aunt Elaine's matchmaking skills proved to be successful. That July, Pat and I spent many evenings sitting around the fire. I really enjoyed the cooler nights when even the heat of the fire was not enough to keep us warm, so we cuddled with a blanket around us as we sat mesmerized by the flames and by one another. There were many times when Pat's mom sent his twin brother Mike out to tell Pat it was late and it was time to come in. We never seemed to run out of things to talk about, so rarely did we notice how late it was getting.

As July came to a close, so did our brief summer romance. I was not yet thinking of Pat and me as an "official couple," but he had a different view of the relationship. The same evening that I returned home from the lake, a guy friend called and invited me to go to a movie. Pat and a group of his friends showed up at the same show. He was not happy to see me there with someone else, and I did not hear from him again. It was actually best for us, since Pat had just graduated from high school, and I was just going into my junior year.

It was July of 1981 when dad hitched our camper to the back of the car and we made our way out to Ten Mile Lake resort for our month long stay. I loved driving along the shore of the lake and following the curve that brought the campground into view. Two years had passed since my brief summer romance with Pat, and it was not on my radar that a romance was going to be rekindled.

I don't remember who struck the first match, but before I knew what was happening, we were once again getting cozy by the fire. Pat, being two years older, was not being told it was late and time to come in. There were many times during that month when the sun was just rising, and we were just saying good night.

Many of our evenings included late-night paddleboat rides. Since the dew of the evening settled on the seats of the paddleboat, I quietly entered our trailer to get a couple towels for us to sit on. My mom was extremely fearful of water and would not have approved of our actions if she had known about them, so I literally was as quiet as a church mouse removing those towels. We paddled out to the middle of the lake and sat and talked for hours.

Pat and I were inseparable that summer, and this time our romance did not end when my parents and I returned home. I made sure not to go on any other dates because I clearly understood that we were a couple. But there were challenges facing us in our relationship.

Our choices of colleges placed many miles between us that fall. For the first month, we communicated by phone, through cards and letters, and occasional visits. While Pat's feelings for me grew, I became restless in the commitment. It was my first year of college, and I was trying to find my way. I shared with Pat that I wanted to go on dates with college friends if I was asked, and I gave him the freedom to do the same. We definitely were not on the same page with this arrangement, so I was faced with an all-or-nothing decision. As much as I did not want to hurt Pat, I made the decision to end our relationship.

My freshman year of college turned out to be a year of incredible spiritual growth for me. I needed Jesus to be my rock because I was still battling feelings of insecurity and low self-esteem. I desired to be in the presence of God, so I attended chapel daily and Wednesday night communion services held on the campus. God graciously gave me a roommate who dearly loved the Lord also, and we fervently prayed together each night before going to sleep. Up until that time, I never knew God so intimately.

When I broke it off with Pat, my calendar was not filled with the dates I hoped I might have. God's plan was for me to date Him that year. My heart had to first be fully His before I could give it away to anyone else. I needed to experience a deep intimacy with the Lord because in a few short months I was going to be thrown into an impenetrable darkness and I needed to draw on the strength I felt while walking in His glorious light.

It was toward the end of my freshman year that I was asked to go on a date by an upperclassman, and it wasn't just any upperclassman. He was well known on campus and held offices in student government. I could hardly believe that he wanted to take me out for dinner. We went to a restaurant called Speak Easy, and I remember my joke was that we truly were able to "speak easy." We continued dating throughout that spring and into the summer.

At about that time, a back injury I had sustained in a car accident when I was ten years old was getting progressively worse. I was in pain from a pinched nerve that ran from the point of the injury down my left leg. It had gotten so bad that I could not sit for very long periods of time, so I decided to see a surgeon in Minneapolis. The young man whom I was dating agreed to go with me to my appointment.

At my doctor's visit, I was told the only course of action to relieve the pain was to fuse the lower three vertebrae in my back. I was only nineteen years old, and the thought of major surgery sent me reeling. Hearing no words of comfort or encouragement from my traveling companion broke my heart, and I felt like the three-hour drive home could not end soon enough so that I could send him on his way.

Ultimately, the heartbreak I experienced over that broken relationship proved to be the best thing that could have happened to me. When I returned home from my appointment, my parents asked if I wanted to go to Ten Mile Steakhouse for dinner, which I readily agreed to.

Walking into the restaurant, I was once again greeted by Pat's penetrating green eyes and welcoming smile. When I saw him, I felt as if my heart were going to leap right out of my chest. As mom and dad sat at the table he directed us to, I lingered back to speak with him for a while. As I told him about my need for surgery, he responded with compassion not only in his voice but also in the way he looked at me.

Here was a man I had devastated by breaking his heart, and he was still able to respond to me with such love and tenderness. I was so undeserving, but yet I was a recipient of his grace. Could I possibly have one more chance at making this work? I was determined to try.

Several days later, we were at the resort again visiting with family. We made plans to go to a restaurant for dinner, and I wanted Pat to be my date. I went to the campground office to see if he was working and learned he had taken a boat out fishing. I asked one of my taunting uncles to take me out in his boat to find my favorite catch.

There he was—boat anchored with fishing line in the water. Be still my heart! My dear uncle pulled his boat alongside Pat's, and somehow it worked for me to (somewhat) gracefully transfer from one boat to another. There we were face-to-face, and I fumbled with my words as I asked him to be my date for the evening. He had every right to say no, and I would have understood, but instead he was willing to put his heart on the line once again.

We had a wonderful evening. In fact, it was like the eight months of separation had not happened. Every time we somehow touched throughout the night, I thought my insides would burst. The butterflies were not only contained to my stomach; I felt the flutter of their wings everywhere. When Pat kissed me good night, I knew he was the treasure I had longed for, and I was grateful to be getting another chance. Our relationship flourished throughout that summer. In the fall, as I went back to college, we were once again separated by miles, but this time, it was only distance separating us. My heart was fully his.

My back condition continued to deteriorate that fall, and I was scheduled for surgery in January of 1983. I moved back home at Christmas break to prepare for the upcoming procedure. Pat's uncle had unexpectedly died from a heart attack months earlier, so he was living at home, also, helping his dad with the resort.

In the first week after the New Year, a surgeon cut away bone in my hip that was pinching the nerve that was causing the pain down my leg, and he used the cutaway bone to fuse my lower vertebrae. The first night after surgery was quite rough. I needed help turning every couple of hours. I needed medicine to control the pain.

Pat stayed by my side the entire first night in the hospital after I had the surgery. He slid a chair up next to my bed and kept his arm on the mattress next to my side so that if he dozed off and I woke up, he would feel my movement and wake up to help me. On the second night, Mom told Pat to go home and get rest; she would stay with me.

My roommate from college made the mistake of bringing a flip chair (a chair that can be folded out into a bed) to the hospital for my mom to lie on. I think it was the best night's sleep my mom ever had. There was no way I could get her to wake up (I've told her she will never live that down, and now it is in writing).

I had to be in the hospital for over a week, and Pat came to my room early each morning and stayed late into the evening. If we were ever going to spend our lives together, he was already proving he was going to hold up his part of the vow to love me in sickness and in health.

I spent the winter months of that year recovering, and since there is not a lot of activity on a summer resort in the dead of winter, Pat and I again were inseparable. He came over to the house every night, and we sat on one couch and mom and dad on the other. Before mom and dad went to bed and before Pat left for home, we watched *All in the Family*. I knew Pat and I were at a new level in our relationship when I joined in singing with Edith Bunker in my mimicking, high-pitched, shaky voice while he unsuccessfully tried covering my mouth to get me to stop. It was the same scenario the next night.

It was in March of that same year when the word *marriage* first entered our vocabulary. We were on a road trip to Kansas City, Missouri, to visit my uncle and matchmaking aunt when we started talking and dreaming about a life together. I was at a pinnacle of happiness, but I was about to be confronted by an enemy that had other plans for me. On that trip, I was once again visited by an oppressive darkness in my mind. I was consumed with condemning thoughts and false accusations.

That spring, even though there was no ring on my finger or an official proposal from Pat, he and I walked through the resort, looking at different living options after we got married. I remember as a little girl I pretended my parents' home was my home, that I was the wife and mom. While I cleaned or helped in the kitchen, my mind was in a make-believe world of homemaking. I always, always, *always* wanted to be a wife and a mom.

It was August before there was a ring on my finger. Pat knew me well enough to know that I wanted to help choose my diamond. As we went from store to store, I felt like we were on a romantic adventure in search of a treasured keepsake from him to me. I don't remember how many rings I tried on, but we finally found the one I deemed perfect.

The ring had to be sized, so it was going to take a week before it could be picked up. I was not about to let him go get that diamond without me. Even though I love surprises, delayed gratification is not one of my strengths. Knowing he had the ring and not knowing when he was going to propose was pushing my limits. If he did have other plans for a proposal, he was willing to forego those in order to make me happy.

We entered the jewelry store on that sunny day in August, and they presented to us a beautiful set of gold bands (engagement and wedding rings together), and I knew that the sparkling diamonds matched the sparkle in our eyes. They fit perfectly. I made the difficult choice of delaying my gratification, and I carefully placed them back in the black felt box while Pat finished the purchase. After leaving the store, Pat and I drove to a nearby park that we often went to while dating. Sitting at a picnic table under the cool shade of a tree, Pat asked me to be his wife. My little girl dreams were coming true. Would this be the fairy tale to end all fairy tales?

The next thirteen months before our wedding were a combination of intense college courses, wedding planning, and an ever-present darkness blanketing my mind. Unresolved identity issues made me fair game to the enemy's accusations. He was not about to let me go into marriage thinking I could be successful as a wife.

I was so glad that Pat chose to attend the same college as I attended that fall. When I felt overwhelmed with fear and anxiety, it was his touch that made me feel safe. When I shared with him the battle going on in my mind, it did not scare him away. He continued to love and support me. I was secure in the identity I had when I was with him.

Our wedding day finally arrived on September 22, 1984. I woke up that morning to rain hitting against my window. I was so disappointed; rain was not a part of my fairy-tale wedding, but by late morning, the sun broke through the clouds and the day could not have been more beautiful. Equally beautiful was how the joy of this day illuminated the darkness of my thoughts. The chains had fallen off, at least for one day.

Pat and I were intentional in letting our guests know that we wanted our marriage centered on Jesus. The scriptures we chose reflected God's view of marriage and what love should look like between a man and wife. The words of each song sung reflected what was in our hearts as we started our lives together.

After a dinner reception at the church, a horse and buggy picked us up, and I got to be Cinderella with my Prince Charming as we rode through the city streets and around beautiful Lake Alice on my special day I had begun dreaming about so very long ago. Sept. 22, 1984, an ordinary day to many, but for Pat and me, this was the beginning of our "happily ever after."

Following a weeklong Caribbean cruise for our honeymoon, Pat and I settled into our new life as husband and wife on the resort. Pat's grandparents' home, centrally located on the property, became our home. The house was dated but had great potential. Built into a hill, it had a walkout basement facing the lake with a tucked-under, single-car garage. The basement was unfinished, so you had to go up a flight of stairs to get to the main living area.

At the top of the stairs was the kitchen with old, grey-speckled linoleum sporting a ten- inch red border around the perimeter. There was also linoleum going halfway up the walls. It had yellowed from the passage of time and had red, intersecting lines creating a large, checked pattern. The cupboards were blonde with retro silver handles and hinges. Today, this kitchen would be well appreciated and sought after, but not in 1984. The best feature was the large windows overlooking the lake and resort.

The living room was about the same size as the kitchen, and the walls were covered in knotty pine. Our newlywed budget allowed us to purchase used furniture that was advertised in our local paper that consisted of two rockers, a hide-a-bed couch, a combined footstool/coffee table, and two end tables. The heavy, exposed wooden frames with the earth-toned tweed fabric complemented the knotty pine walls, and I was pleased with the atmosphere we created on a limited budget.

On the wall opposite the couch stood an old TV stand on wheels that held our 27-inch television complete with rabbit ears sticking out the top, picking up the signal of three stations. We never watched a clear screen. We could see a picture in the background, but it was like watching it through falling snow. I was constantly moving those rabbit ears around, trying to get a clearer picture.

Claiming a spot on one of those used end tables was our party line telephone. When someone called, the phone rang at the resort, at my in-laws, and at our home. If the resort office/steakhouse was open, I had to wait for them to answer, and then I could pick up the receiver and listen in to see if the call was for me.

If by some slim chance it was, I could never talk long because we could not tie up the business phone, nor could I make many calls because the majority of people I wanted to call were long distance, and it was too expensive. It took me awhile, but I eventually convinced Pat that we should get our own private line. I never cease to be amazed at how often people are slow to make changes because that is how it has always been.

The living room had large windows with the same view as the kitchen, overlooking the lake and the resort. We had a view of the sandy beach where children splashed in the water while mothers bathed in the sun. We could see the fishermen pulling their boats up to the dock and watch as they walked with their stringer of fish to the cleaning house. At night, we could see the glow of campground fires outside cabins and campers, and when our windows were open, we could hear the laughter of family and friends as they enjoyed time together.

Off of the living room were two bedrooms and a bath. This completed our ever so small yet ever so cozy love nest.

We eventually remodeled, adding more living area downstairs for the three children the Lord blessed us with.

In the midst of all the joy that home brought to our family, I continued to battle an unseen enemy for the first several years of our married life. Even though I was in close fellowship with Jesus, I was struggling because I did not know who I was in Christ, nor did I fully understand what it meant to be a child of God.

Chapter 4
Who Is the Woman in the Mirror?

On calm days, Ten Mile Lake was like glass, reflecting the beauty of its surroundings. Standing on the dock, I could look into the water and see my own reflection; it was like looking into a mirror. The image the water cast was fairly accurate, but just the slightest breeze formed ripples on the water, distorting my reflected image. I could not look at that distorted image for very long because the constant movement of the water made me nauseous.

As a young child, I paid little attention to the image I saw in the mirror when I got ready for school in the morning. It didn't matter to me that I looked practically bald from the front when my thin blonde hair was pulled back in a ponytail. It didn't matter that my legs were chubbier than some of my friends. It didn't bother me if I could not run as fast, jump as high, or sing as beautiful as someone else. I liked the young girl I saw in the mirror.

I remember as a child attending the county fair and going into the Fun House, which contained mirrors offering a distorted view of reality. A gently curved, concave mirror made me look extremely thin while a convex curved mirror made me look as wide as I was tall. I could easily laugh at the reflected images because I knew they did not accurately represent me.

As I got older, however, my naiveté about beauty and success was challenged as I started seeing how the world around me defined them. If I believed what I was seeing, then my thin hair, chubby legs, and off-key voice were not, by the world's definition, acceptable. A new voice was speaking to my world, and the messages were being communicated through TV, billboards, magazines, and the people in my life. Each source had an idea of who I should strive to be, and I quickly came to recognize the areas of my life where I did not measure up to the world's standards. The untainted image I once had of myself was quickly becoming distorted by the winds of public opinion.

In both junior and senior high school, I found myself envying the girls with thick, long hair. I now loathed my legs because my calves ran from my knees all the way to my ankles, and I even discovered there was a name for that; I had *cankles*. Yes, there is a definition: "a thickened area between the calf and the ankle obscuring where one ends and the other begins."[1] I never saw a woman with cankles featured on the front of a magazine. I concluded that my legs had to be covered as much as possible.

I also did not want to expose my arms. The women I saw in pictures had thin arms. Mine looked like I either lifted weights or was raised on a farm where I spent my days moving hay bales. Neither was true. It was how God made me, with muscular, contoured arms. There are many women today who work hard for that look, but it wasn't considered attractive when I was growing up.

I have always had a full-length mirror to look into when getting dressed for the day. I cannot count the number of times I was satisfied with what I was wearing only to walk into the bathroom and see myself in different lighting in a different mirror and quickly do a 180 to return to my closet to make a new choice. I didn't need anyone else in the room to answer the question, "Do these pants make my butt look big?" The mirror doesn't lie…right?

Why is it that I believed one mirror over another? Why is it that early in life, I adopted the world's definition of physical beauty? How I perceived myself outwardly was no match for the battle I was facing on the inside. I was falling apart because everything I had based my identity on was falling apart. I was letting everything and everyone define me. I was listening to the wrong voices.

When we compare ourselves to the people in our lives and those we see in the media, it doesn't take a rocket scientist to tell us where we fall short. Our drive to be accepted is so strong that we will go to great lengths to measure up to the world's definition of success and beauty. The following story is an extreme example, but I'm guessing that many of us have done ridiculous things to fit in.

> Three women, two younger and one senior citizen, were sitting naked in a sauna. Suddenly, there was a beeping sound. The first young woman pressed her forearm and the beeping stopped. The others looked at her questioningly. "That was my pager, she said. I have a microchip under the skin of my arm."
>
> A few minutes later, a phone rang. The second young woman lifted her palm to her ear. When she finished, she explained, "That was my mobile phone. I have a microchip in my hand."
>
> The older woman felt very low tech. Not to be outdone, she decided she had to do something just as impressive. She stepped out of the sauna

> and went to the bathroom. She returned with a piece of toilet paper hanging from her backside.
>
> The two others raised their eyebrows and stared at her. The older woman finally said, "Well, will you look at that. I'm receiving a fax."[2]

We idolize the rich and famous. Success is often determined by the amount of money in our bank accounts, the number of friends we have following us on Facebook, the titles that precede or follow our names, by our status in a community, and if we are beautiful according to the world's standards. If toilet paper hanging from our backsides gets us recognition and admiration from others, then show us the nearest bathroom.

When someone asks, "Who are you?" there are a number of ways we can answer that question. Before my junior year in high school, I could have identified myself in one of these ways: "I'm Lisa. I'm a cheerleader. I'm a basketball player. I'm class president. I'm popular. I'm well liked." How self-absorbed I was to think I could identify myself in those ways! However, every one of those was subject to change, and change they did.

Embarrassment over my cankles kept me out of a cheerleading skirt. A back injury ended my basketball career. A poor decision on my part alienated me from friends, so there was no more being voted class president or making the cut in the yearbook of those who made the senior class hall of fame. The very things that I believed defined me as a person were crumbling, and I became easy prey for the enemy. If I didn't know who I was, he was more than willing to fill my mind with his ideas for my identity.

The Bible describes Satan in this way, "He was a murderer from the beginning; not holding to the truth for there is no truth in him. When he lies he speaks his native language, for he is a liar and the father of lies" (John 8:44). Satan's number-one weapon in the life of a believer is deception. He cannot read our minds, but he can implant thoughts, ideas, and falsehoods in us, which he often disguises as being our own thoughts. He knows that if he strategically places lies in our minds and we believe them, he can then control our lives with those lies.

The Bible gives two powerful examples of this tactic of Satan. The first is found at the very beginning of mankind when Satan spoke to Eve in the Garden of Eden. "Now the serpent was more crafty than any of the wild animals the Lord God had made. He said to the woman, 'Did God really say, you must not eat from any tree in the garden?' …You will not surely die. For God knows that when you eat of it your eyes will be opened, and you will be like God, knowing good and evil" (Gen. 3:1-5).

Satan cleverly deceived Eve into questioning God and then presented her with an offer she could not refuse. She didn't have to be known as Eve, the wife of Adam, the keeper of God's garden. She could be like God! She was willing to trade a seemingly insignificant identity for one of power, wisdom, and control. She believed Satan's lie, and we have our first human identity crisis. When Adam and Eve sinned, they immediately experienced fear and shame and no longer knew who they were as children of God.

Our second powerful example is found in John 13:2, "The evening meal was being served, and the Devil had already prompted Judas Iscariot, son of Simon, to betray Jesus." Satan knew Judas well enough to know that money and status were important to him. Judas wanted to be identified with Jesus if it meant being given an important position in the kingdom he thought Jesus was going to establish.

When Judas realized the kingdom Jesus was talking about was neither physical nor political but it was a spiritual kingdom, he knew he would not obtain the status he was looking for, so he betrayed Jesus in order to receive money and favor from the religious leaders. Judas embraced Satan's lie and the end result? Judas had a worldly sorrow (see 2 Cor. 7:10) that led to his death when he took his own life.

The enemy wanted to keep me ignorant of my true identity in Christ. I was a threat to his kingdom, and he hated me. If he could mess up my thinking by convincing me—which he so often did—that I was unlovable, unacceptable, and insignificant, then he could keep me from being effective for the kingdom of God.

I had wounded places in my life, and the enemy went to work formulating lies around those wounded places. As I previously pointed out, Satan disguises his lies as our own thoughts. The words spoken to me, "You know what those Ferber girls are like," were translated in my mind as, "I'm not good enough. I'm not acceptable." When my act of indiscretion toward a friend resulted in lost relationships, this is what my mind heard: "nobody likes me; I can never be a good friend to anyone; I'm all alone and nobody cares."

After meeting and falling in love with Pat, I found my identity in him. He loved me, accepted me, and wanted to spend time with me. I felt complete when I was with him. Did you catch those words, "when I was with him?" When I was alone, however, I could not shut off the barrage of condemning thoughts and accusations. Eventually, I could not shut them off even when I was with Pat.

When the enemy gets his foot in the door to our thoughts, he is never satisfied remaining at the door. He wants full access and will stop at nothing to get in. Not knowing how to handle my insecurities opened up the door to irrational fears and demonic oppression.

I felt I had no control over my mind. The best way to describe what I was experiencing is by defining the word *oppression,* which is a feeling of being weighed down in mind or body through a cruel exercise of power. There was a persistent pressure of thought that said I was going to fail as a wife and mother, and it would destroy my Christian witness. This penetrating darkness consumed me, and I questioned if I were ever going to be free.

For a long time, I kept silent about the war being waged in my mind. There were very few people I allowed into this intense time of suffering. In my twisted way of thinking, I believed that to be vulnerable and expose that Lisa did not have it all together risked being rejected, and that terrified me. I had been down that path too many times.

Pat was someone, however, who I felt safe to share my feelings with. He was my rock. When the haunting, nagging thoughts of the enemy were next to unbearable, he was there to hold me. He was to me what David was to King Saul in the Old Testament. When a tormenting spirit of fear and depression troubled King Saul, he called for David, and David played music on his harp. This helped Saul feel better, and the tormenting spirit went away.

Pat was my harp. He knew when darkness was heavy on my spirit, and it was his words and gentle touch that gave me hope that things would get better, and things actually did get better. Sometime during our first year of marriage, the accusing voices went silent. My thoughts were my own once again, and I relished in the peace that I had.

Our precious first baby was due at the end of October in 1986. While the excitement, anticipation, and preparation for the baby consumed us, Satan once again had me on his menu.

Luke 11:24-27 reads: "When an evil spirit comes out of a man, it goes through arid places seeking rest and does not find it." Then it says, "I will return to the house I left." When it arrives, it finds the house swept clean and put in order. Then it goes and takes seven other spirits more wicked than itself, and they go in and live there. And the final condition of that man is worse than the first."

I do not believe that an evil spirit can possess a born-again child of God, but I do believe we can allow one to take up residence in our thoughts and actions. I had previously given the enemy a place in my thoughts. When he left the habitation of my mind, I left the place he had occupied empty. I had not answered the question, "Who Is the woman in the mirror?" I was fair game for him to return.

One month before I gave birth to Benjamin, that familiar presence of evil did return. Once again, I felt I had no control over the darkness shrouding my thoughts that I would morally fail as a wife and mother. The only reprieve I got was during labor when that was the only thing I could focus on. Joy was able to fill my heart, however, when the doctor announced I had given birth to a baby boy.

He was so perfect, and my lifelong dream of being a mom had come true, but the change in my hormones after his birth, accompanied by the enemy's relentless taunts, spiraled me into a state of deep despair. I was in full-blown postpartum depression. The scripture was true; my final condition was worse than the first.

God blessed me with a child whom I affectionately called Rip Van Winkle because he was such a good sleeper. That was exactly what I needed as I was in such a horrible place mentally and emotionally. I needed time to read the Word of God and any other books that brought peace to my troubled mind. I did not seek any medical help, which I now regret, but I felt the best thing for Ben was my breast milk, so I did not want to be on any medication.

I can honestly say that I never lived with a sense of mental peace for the next seven years. My friends and family members never knew because I was able to hide it well. It was during this time I became proficient at wearing different masks to disguise my pain, so what people saw on the outside did not match what I was feeling on the inside. My masks did exactly what I wanted them to do, which was to make it appear as though I had it all together. I functioned in life just fine, but that deep, indescribable mental torment was a constant companion.

In 1993, I was in a bookstore, and my eyes were drawn to a book entitled, *The Bondage Breaker*, by Dr. Neil T. Anderson. A picture of a linked chain was on the cover with the center link broken. The words on the front cover were like a flashing light, signaling hope. They read, "Overcoming negative thoughts, irrational feelings, and habitual sins."

A sense of hope and anticipation filled my spirit as I read these words on the back cover:

> **You're trapped**. You don't know how you ended up in such a mess – locked in habits you can't seem to break or caught in sin. You're a Christian and this sort of thing doesn't happen to Christians…or so you've been told. **You are not alone**. The Bible warns repeatedly that all Christians will struggle against Satan and his spiritual forces of darkness. While the spiritual conflict that churns within you is very real, the answers are just as tangible.
> *The Bondage Breaker* reveals the whys and hows of spiritual warfare **and exposes Satan's battle for your mind**. *The Bondage Breaker* shares the

> powerful truth that will break even the most stubborn habits or private sins. **You can live life without chains!** Don't wait any longer to discover that your most important defense against a life of bondage is recognizing the enemy and knowing how to defeat him.[3]

I could not get my money out fast enough to buy this book. Within days of my purchase, I was in my pastor's office and noticed a flyer on his desk with a picture of Neil Anderson. He was going to be the keynote speaker at a conference in Minneapolis, Minnesota. I could hardly believe it. I immediately registered for that conference. God's hand of deliverance was taking hold of mine.

I know that Dr. Anderson was speaking powerful truths that weekend, but the one truth that will forever be etched in my memory was what God spoke to my heart. As I sat in the church sanctuary, I heard from God. It was not an audible voice, but it was just as real to me as the opposing voice of torment. I heard these words, "One day I will use you to help others be free." I wept like a baby and in my heart said, "God, how could you ever use me. I am such a mess."

God was in the process of turning my mess into a message; the message would be birthed in my rebirth. In a season of intense suffering, I found me, and I found the answer to the question, "Who is the woman in the mirror?" Discovering the answer to that question would be the key to my surviving Pat's death and making the choice to keep living.

God used my days of darkness to produce my qualities of perseverance, character, and hope. He saw the day when the music of Pat's life that ministered to my spirit was silenced, and He knew that I needed to be secure not in what is changeable, but in the One who is the same yesterday, today, and forever. Like a pilgrim who travels to a sacred place, I was on my journey to freedom.

Chapter 5
A Journey to Freedom

Coming to the realization that your identity has been based on lies you believed does not automatically erase those lies. It would be so nice if we could push the delete button and choose a new, blank document and start our story over. In reality, starting a new chapter in an existing story and learning how to embrace the previous chapters is a necessary part of our journey.

I had many days of wrestling with God as I walked through my season of darkness. I often asked Him why I was in such an intense time of mental suffering. I looked at other believers and often wished I was like them. I was under the impression that they were not fighting their own demons. How wrong I was.

In my fight to be free, I discovered I was not the only believer wearing a mask. Others who were also struggling with obsessive thoughts and a faulty perception of self surrounded me. It was not only true for me but for numerous other believers that you can be saved and have the Holy Spirit living within you and still live a defeated life.

Satan wants to convince us that the Christian life doesn't work, that God's Word really is not true and nothing significantly changed when we surrendered our lives to Christ. He will do anything he can to distract us from believing the truth about who we are in Christ because he does not want us to live free. This is confirmed in John 10:10

where it says, "The thief (Satan) comes only to kill, steal, and destroy."

Add to Satan's lies our own self-sufficiency, and we have a recipe for disaster. Placing our confidence in our intelligence, our appearance, or our accomplishments instead of in God will never result in lasting peace. All of these strengths will eventually fade, and we will be left battling the demons of destruction.

Proverbs 23:7 is a verse that speaks of the power a person's thoughts has over a person's behavior. It reads, "For as he thinks within himself, so he is" (NASB).

If you were constantly told as a child that you would never amount to anything or that you could not do anything right, and you believed it to be true, that would affect your sense of identity and subsequent behavior. You would not be eager to try something new, and if you did, you certainly wouldn't believe you'd succeed.

On the other hand, if you were constantly affirmed and encouraged and told you could accomplish anything, and you believed that to be true, there would be no stopping you. Even if you did fail, you would not be afraid to try again.

When Satan attacks the mind of a believer, he doesn't speak his lies just once. As long as we cooperate with him, he continues to push the play button on his implanted recorded message. As we continue to listen and entertain the statements played over and over in our minds, a stronghold is built.

Second Corinthians 10:5 describes a *stronghold* as an "argument or pretention that sets itself up against the knowledge of God." A stronghold is something that has such a tight grip on us that it consumes our thinking, our actions, and our attitudes.

This was definitely true in my life. Because I entertained Satan's lies and allowed them to dictate my thoughts, they robbed me of the abundant living that was promised to me in the second half of John 10:10: "I (Jesus) have come that you might have life and have it to the full."

I felt both overpowered and controlled by my self-destructive thinking. So much of my energy and mental focus was spent dwelling on lies about my identity. I allowed them to be bigger and more powerful than God in my life. I even allowed Pat to be bigger than God.

Every other fall, Pat went on a ten-day hunting trip out of state. My parents only lived fifteen miles away, but I packed up the children and moved to their home for those ten days. It was a wonderful opportunity for the children and me to stay at my mom and dad's, but it was also a place I felt safe in the midst of my haunting thoughts. I felt lost when I was away from Pat.

A key verse in *Freedom In Christ Ministries* is John 8:32: "Then you will know the truth and the truth will set you free." I heard at the Living Free in Christ conference that for every lie that holds you captive, there is a truth that sets you free, and embracing this was the first step in my journey toward freedom. I started down a path in search of the truth that would release me from my chains of bondage.

Second Corinthians 10:3-5 reads, "For though we live in the world, we do not wage war as the world does. The weapons we fight with are not the weapons of the world. On the contrary, they have divine power to demolish strongholds." I had been waging war as the world did—finding my identity in my appearance, my abilities, my accomplishments, and in my husband.

In Psalm 107:13-14, I read: "Then they cried out to the LORD in their trouble, and He saved them from their distress.

He brought them out of darkness and the deepest gloom and broke away their chains." My victory began with a cry for help. I was not delivered instantly from my fears and insecurities. Some do experience instant freedom, but I believe they are the exception. True freedom requires hard work. It is not a walk in the park. I cried out to God when I came to the end of me and when I realized I was powerless on my own and that I needed His strength to help me get through the layers of deception.

As I have already established, the mind is the battlefield. When someone says, "It's all in your head," they are exactly right, because what is going on in your head is very real. If I was going to win the battle for my mind, I had to do what 1 Peter 1:13 says and that was to "Prepare my mind for action" (NLT). This was a war I could not sit back and be passive about.

The first unwavering truth that I had to accept was that Jesus had already won the battle for me when He defeated Satan on the cross. First John 3:8 is Christ's mission statement; "The reason the Son of God appeared was to destroy the devil's work." Colossians 2:15 tells how this was done, "And having disarmed the powers and authorities, He made a public spectacle of them, triumphing over them by the cross." Christ stripped Satan of his battle armor and his weapons. He was rendered a defeated foe.

With one defeating blow, Christ had nullified the power of Satan's lies in my life. Did you hear me? Just one defeating blow. This was true even though it was not yet working out in my reality. This leads to the second truth that I had to embrace before I was victorious. I had to believe the positional truth I had in Christ found in Colossians 1:13: "For He has rescued us *(me)* from the dominion of darkness and brought us *(me)* into the kingdom of the Son He loves" (*emphasis mine*). When the darkness was so dark, as it was in different seasons of my life, I needed to allow the brilliant light and life of Jesus to penetrate my darkness, and that would come as I renewed my mind.

One of the first things I did after attending the Living Free in Christ conference was to schedule a time to go through *The Seven Steps to Freedom* designed by Dr. Neil Anderson.

Two precious women sat over five hours with me as I worked through *The Steps*. One gently led me, and the other prayed.

The Steps are a comprehensive process that helped me to resolve my personal and spiritual conflicts. There were things in my past that needed to be dealt with before I could find my freedom, and much of my past was dealt with through repentance and forgiveness. First John 1:9 says, "If we confess our sins, God is faithful and just to forgive us our sins and to cleanse us from all unrighteousness."

I had given the enemy access to areas of my life through false guidance, rebellion, pride, and deeds of the flesh (see Galatians 6). I confessed these areas before God and my two witnesses and I accepted His forgiveness. I also discovered through this process that I was in bondage to bitterness over past words and actions that had produced a negative impact on my life. I needed to genuinely forgive those who had wronged me both intentionally and unintentionally. I also needed to forgive myself for the times I messed up. I not only forgave with words, I forgave from my heart.

The Steps put me on the path of reclaiming the promise of freedom that Christ had purchased for me with His shed blood. They were instrumental in helping me understand how the enemy had woven together painful events in my life and strategically formulated lies that seemed, in my mind, to be true because of traumas I had previously experienced.

The cleansing that took place in this session made me ready to dismantle the web of lies that had been dominating my life. *Praise God!* A light was peering into my darkness. My freedom appointment was a one-day event, but the renewing of my mind took months. I didn't get to my place of captivity overnight. The fortress of lies had to be pulled down brick by brick, or more appropriately, truth by truth.

Lies are not always easy to recognize. *Amen!* If the promises of God's word were going to heal my mind, then I needed to know the wrong things I believed, so I asked God to help me identify what thoughts were true and which ones were lies. He instructed me to hold them to the standard of His word. If a thought was in agreement with the word of God, it was a true thought, and if it wasn't, it was a lie no matter how true it felt. Lies took my focus off of God. They were distracting and defeating, and my entire being quickly responded to falsehoods with fear and anxiety.

Jesus was my ultimate example of how He used the word of God to silence the enemy's taunts. In Luke 4, we learn how the Spirit led Jesus into the desert where He fasted for forty days, and at the end of those forty days, the enemy was there to tempt Him to sin. It is important to note that Satan came to Jesus at a vulnerable time. He was hungry and had definite physical needs after going without food for that many days.

First Peter 5:8 speaks of Satan as a roaring lion seeking someone to devour. Lions often prey on animals that are weak, sick, and isolated. Jesus, being fully human at this point, had to have felt weak from lack of nutrition, and He was certainly isolated out there in the desert, but He was not ignorant of Satan's schemes.

For every temptation that Satan placed before Him, Jesus responded, "It is written," and then quoted appropriate scripture that disarmed the enemy's lie. Two things became apparent to me: first Jesus spoke out loud, and second, what He spoke was the word of God. The reason Jesus spoke out loud is because Satan does not have the ability to read our minds.

At one time in my life, I might have argued that it seems as though he can read our minds, but that was before I learned it's because he put the thought there in the first place. I made up my mind then and there to speak the truth, out loud, over my life. Jesus had given me divine instruction on how to win the battle.

When the thought came that God had abandoned me, I quoted His word that says, "He will never leave me nor forsake me," (Deuteronomy 31:6) and "nothing can separate me from the love of God" (Romans 8:39).

When I was afraid and felt like I was losing all soundness of mind, I proclaimed, "God has not given me a spirit of fear, but of power, love and a sound mind," (2 Timothy 1:7 KJV) and "I have the mind of Christ" (1 Corinthians 2:16).

When feeling unloved, I recited, "God loves me with an everlasting love" (Jeremiah 31:3). When feeling worthless, I remembered, "God had ***chosen me*** before the foundation of the world" (Ephesians 1:4). When feeling like an unworthy friend, I reminded myself, "I am Christ's friend" (John 15:15).

When Satan bombarded me with nagging and haunting thoughts that I would fail as a wife and ruin my Christian witness, I spoke the truth that God had created us male and female. It was God's plan from the beginning that man's loneliness would be met in his wife and the two would become one flesh. God's calling on my life was to be Pat's wife and to fulfill this call in the strength of God. I would not fail.

Early on in my battle, God gave me a promise in Isaiah 54:14, "In righteousness you will be established; you will be far from oppression, for you will not fear; and from terror, for it will not come near you" (NASB). I was given this promise before I even knew how to do battle using the Word of God. In my ignorance I held onto it, at times only by my fingertips, but I did hold on.

When I started believing what God said about me in His word rather than believing my thoughts and feelings, I found freedom. Galatians 5:1 confirmed that it was for freedom that Christ had set me free, and after being set free, I needed to stand firm and not be burdened again by a yoke of slavery. I needed to guard against falling back into controlling thoughts. The way the Bible instructed me to do this was by taking captive every thought and making it obedient to Christ (2 Corinthians 10:5).

When a stranger comes to your door, are you cautious about letting the stranger in? What if this stranger is trying to sell you something? Are you quick to buy, or do you take time to research the product?

When a thought comes knocking at the door of my mind, I need to immediately determine if I'm going to let that thought cross the threshold and enter. A litmus test that I like to use is Philippians 4:8, "Finally my brothers, whatever is true, whatever is noble, whatever is right, whatever is pure, whatever is lovely, whatever is admirable—if anything is excellent or praiseworthy—think about such things."

If the thought passes the test, I'm free to welcome it and think on it. If it fails the test, I need to immediately slam the door on the intruder in order to protect what is rightfully mine—a sound mind. Choosing a right thought shuts the door. This is what it means to take every thought captive.

Before I was familiar with *pop-ups* on a computer (which are basically ads that pop up on your computer screen enticing you to click on them), I ignorantly introduced viruses into my laptop by clicking on the pop-ups. Viruses are designed to perform some type of harmful activity such as stealing hard disk space, accessing private information, corrupting data, and even rendering the computer useless. Once the virus had infected my computer, I needed help getting it removed.

As Apple is to the world of antivirus, the Word of God is to the mind of the Christian. Our mind is the computer, and Satan's lies, accusations, and falsehoods are the corrupting viruses. As crucial as it is to protect our computers with antivirus software, it is even more critical that we protect our minds with the antivirus software of God's Word. I want you to know, precious reader, it really is true. For every lie that holds you captive, there undeniably is a truth that sets you free.

As I fought for my freedom, a major portion of my time had to be spent renewing my mind with scriptures that confirmed my identity in Christ. I was determined to refute every tongue that accused me (Isaiah 54:17). I prayed, "God help me to see me the way you see me. Help me to believe I am who you say that I am." Verses that were once considered familiar were now life changing as I *chose* to believe them, and they transformed my mind as I spoke them out loud.

- "I am part of a chosen people, a royal priesthood, a holy nation, a people belonging to God, that I may declare the praises of Him who called me out of darkness into His wonderful light" (1 Peter 2:9-10). I am chosen by God to be His very own, and my value comes from being His child. I have worth because of what He has done and not because of what I have done.
- "I am a child of God" (1 John 3:1; John 1:12). These are powerful verses when you

understand that being a child of God means you've inherited the very things of God: significance, safety, security, a sense of belonging.

- "I am Christ's friend" (John 15:15). This was a liberating truth for me! If Jesus wanted me to be His friend, I had all the qualities needed to be a good friend for anyone.
- "I am righteous and holy" (Ephesians 2:24). It isn't what I do or think that makes me holy. It is what Christ did for me on the cross that gives me this status.
- "I am chosen by God and He dearly loves me" (Colossians 3:12; 1 Thessalonians 1:4). Because He dearly loves me, I want to live my life pleasing Him, and that is possible because of His choosing me to be His child.
- "I am born of God and the devil cannot touch me" (1 John 5:18). I did not always know or believe Satan had no power over me. It was so freeing to learn the only way he could influence me was if I allowed him to, and I did not need to allow it.
- "I died with Christ and died to sin ruling my life" (Romans 6:1-6). I obviously did not die physically or I would not be writing this book. I'm united with God through faith, which has freed me from sin because Christ broke the power of sin through His death. Sin and temptation will always be present, but it is my choice whether or not to participate.
- "I am free from any condemning thoughts against me" (Romans 8:1). This includes thoughts in my own mind or from any outside

source. Because my sin died with Christ, I am no longer condemned. If I were standing in a court of law, on the basis of Christ's work on the cross, I would be declared not guilty. Satan however wants me to remain stuck in guilt.

- "I have been given the mind of Christ" (I Corinthians 2:16). In other words, *I'm not going crazy!*
- "I have been crucified with Christ and it is no longer I living but it is Christ living in me" (Galatians 2:20). Translation: when God looks at me, He sees me as if I had died, been buried, and been raised with Jesus. I have become One with Christ. I'm so glad I'm not living life on my own. His victory is my victory.
- "I get to approach God boldly and with freedom and confidence" (Ephesians 3:12). In the Old Testament, this was not the case. Only the Priest could go before God after He was ceremonially cleansed. Because of Jesus, our High Priest, every believer has immediate access to the Father. I can talk with Him about everything and not be afraid to approach Him because I am His child.
- "I am rescued from Satan's rule and I am transferred to the kingdom of Christ (Colossians 1:13)." I don't have to listen to the lies of the enemy. I can choose truth.
- "I am indwelled by Christ Himself. He lives in me" (Colossians 1:27). God's plan was to have His Son live in the hearts of all who believe in Him. Even in my loneliness, I'm never alone, and this is a great comfort to me.

- "I am totally complete in Christ" (Colossians 2:10). I lack nothing for living a life of freedom and joy![1]

A stronghold of the mind left unchecked can become a stronghold of behavior. Behaviors start as thoughts. Nothing pleases Satan more than for us to get entrenched in destructive habits.

The world tends to define us by our behaviors. We do the same thing when we tend to identify ourselves by our habits or strongholds; I'm an alcoholic, a drug addict, a food addict, a liar, a thief, an adulterer, a homosexual.

As a child of God, you have no business identifying yourself in any of these ways. First Corinthians 6:9-11 states,

> Do you not know that the wicked will not inherit the kingdom of God? Do not be deceived: Neither the sexually immoral nor idolaters nor adulterers nor male prostitutes nor homosexual offenders nor thieves not the greedy nor drunkards nor slanderers nor swindlers will inherit the kingdom of God.
>
> And that is what some of you ***were*** *(emphasis mine)***.** But you were washed, you were sanctified, you were justified in the name of the Lord Jesus Christ and by the Spirit of our God.

God sees us for who we are in Christ. He never gives up on us. No matter how long we have struggled and to whatever degree we have failed Him and others in our lives, He sticks beside us until we are free. God always leads us in triumph, and we have to believe that no weapon formed against us will prosper (see Isaiah 54:17).

I chose to think victoriously. I chose to speak victoriously. I chose to pray victoriously. I chose to see myself walking victoriously. As I did, it worked out in my experience, and I lived victoriously. "God calmed the storm to a whisper and stilled the waves. What a blessing was that stillness" (Psalm 107:29-30 NLT).

Somewhere in the process, I no longer clung to the identity of being the wife of Pat Schultz. I was the redeemed, chosen, loved friend, and child of God who was privileged to be Pat's wife. So, on the day he died, I did not lose my identity, and in the difficult days that followed, I still knew who I was, and that gave me the courage to grieve with hope. I was separated from Pat and the pain was unbearable, but it was the same pain that inseparably united me with Jesus.

Chapter 6
The Labor Room of Sorrow

After the paramedics told us that Pat was gone, cries from the depths of our beings erupted from each of us. Jared and I lay on the hard ground embracing one another as we wept, the stones on the pavement leaving imprints on our cheeks. I remember being covered with a blanket, which seems strange on a summer day, but maybe the paramedics feared we would go into shock. Time suddenly stood still, and life went into slow motion.

Genesis 2:21-24 describes how God created Eve by taking a rib from Adam's side while he slept. Adam's response when he awoke and saw Eve was, "This is now bone of my bones and flesh of my flesh; she shall be called woman for she was taken out of man." In essence, Adam was saying that Eve was a part of him. In marriage, a man and a woman join their lives, and the two are seen as one in the eyes of God.

At the moment of Pat's death, I felt part of me left with him. My flesh was being torn apart. If I were to survive, I needed to bring to mind the things I still believed about God. Many of those beliefs would be worked out in the days and weeks to follow, but immediately I needed to hold onto the truth that God was with the children and me, and He would not abandon us in our time of need. Colossians 1:17 reads, "He is before all things, and in Him all things hold together." God ***would*** hold us together.

The ambulance attendant told me they were taking Pat to a local funeral home in Park Rapids. Did I really hear that correctly? You are taking my husband to a funeral home? I told Tim I wanted to go there, which was a strange request for me to make since I did not want to see Pat's body. But God was at work, and there was a message from the Lord that would come from the mouth of the funeral director.

When I met him, he looked at me and said, "Lisa," and then he quoted this verse from 1 Corinthians 2:9: "Eye has not seen, ear has not heard, nor has the mind conceived what the Lord has for those who love Him." Those words proved to be prophetic. At that moment though nothing made sense, a day would come when I would see and hear how Pat's death impacted the lives of others. My mind would understand how God was using this tragedy for our good and His glory.

With the convenience of cell phones, within moments of Pat's accident, prayers were reaching the throne room of God on our behalf. One of the first people called was our pastor. He was at our denominations family camp when he heard the news. He shared with the believers there that our family needed prayers. A pastor at the camp by the name of Jim Comfort prostrated himself on the ground while he made intercession for us. I like to believe there were stones imprinting his cheeks simultaneously with Jared and me. The real beauty in it was that God chose a man with the last name of Comfort to pray for our comfort.

After receiving the call, my pastor and his wife immediately left the family camp to come to Jared and me. He originally thought he was driving me to Minneapolis to meet up with Pat at North Memorial Trauma Center. But as we know, that was not to be. We still made arrangements, however, to meet in town along the route where Jared, Cindy, and I got into their vehicle to make the final trek home.

As we drove, my mind was having a difficult time comprehending how a few short hours before we were laughing and Pat was by my side, and now I was returning home without him. My day could be summed up in the words of Naomi in Ruth 1:21: "I went away full, but the Lord has brought me back empty." I left home that morning married and whole. I was returning home widowed and broken.

As I sat in the seat behind Pastor Steve, I could hear his quiet sobs. He loved Pat like the rest of us, and he was not only feeling the pain of our loss but of his loss as well. Jeanna, his wife, took her hand, reached back, and gently placed it on my leg. There was no talking during those moments. There were no words to ease the pain we were all feeling, yet I felt strangely comforted by the silence. My children and I would not be walking through the valley of the shadow of death alone. However, the magnitude of what just happened had not fully settled in.

The enemy had not forgotten my previous strongholds, and he wasted no time trying to capitalize on my emotional vulnerability. Don't ever underestimate how evil the enemy is. He preys on our weakest moments. His agenda is for our destruction, and he will use any situation to his advantage. A familiar darkness hovered over me in the car that day trying to lure me into believing I had lost my identity now that Pat was gone. Insecurity and fear were knocking at the door of my mind. Would I let them in?

Even in the midst of despair, my mind was ready for action, and I was able to take my thoughts captive. My identity issue had long been settled and as blessed as I was to be the wife of Pat, this role did not define me. As I said before, if it had, who was I now that he was gone? I was still Lisa, child of God, friend of Jesus, ***bride*** of Christ. I was free to grieve with a sound mind.

As we drove, my heart was breaking for my two children at home as they longed for my embrace and were dealing with the reality that their dad was not coming home. I knew they had family surrounding them as they waited for me, but my mother's heart was telling me that no one could take my place. They needed me and I needed them. As we pulled in the driveway at Pat's parents' home, Ben and Jenna fell into my arms. My pain intensified as their sobs filled my ears. My heart cried out, "Lord Jesus, help me. How do I walk this unchartered journey?"

Throughout the evening, friends and family kept arriving. One by one, they embraced me, all struggling as they tried to wrap their minds around the fact Pat was gone. At one point, I lay in a fetal position on the floor as the grief I was feeling overwhelmed me. I heard others crying. I heard prayers spoken. I was physically there but mentally I felt as though I were watching a scene from a movie I did not want to be a part of.

I knew I still had to go home that evening and face a penetrating emptiness. Everything would be as we left it that morning—Pat's shoes by the door, his jacket hanging on the hook in the back hall, the towel he had used that morning still hanging to dry. I would have to look at our bed where intimate moments had been shared, never to be shared again. I would have to look at his clothes still hanging in our closet, knowing I would never see him in that favorite denim shirt, tattered through years of wear. I would have to look at the table where we shared meals as a family and see an empty chair never to be filled by him again. Once more my heart was pleading, "Jesus, help me."

My family and friends were so ready and wanting to minister to the children and me in any way they could. We were not going home alone. My sisters and two girlfriends came to spend the night with us so they could attend to our needs. My typical, independent nature was set aside, and I readily embraced the caring hands of others.

It was important that my children saw in me an unshakable trust in God. When we had time alone, I said to them, "Jesus will be lifted up in this tragedy, and we will grieve, but we will not grieve as those who have no hope." Our hope rested in the truth that we would see their daddy again. He knew Jesus Christ as his Lord and Savior, and we would be reunited in Heaven. My most important task from that moment on was to model before my children a trust and confidence in God that was unshakable, but at the same time, being very real in my grief so they could be real in theirs.

Even though it was late and we were all emotionally drained, Ben grabbed his fishing gear and went down to the resort. He made his way out to the point, the same place where I had met his dad on a moonlit night twenty-four years earlier. He needed time to process what had taken place. Like his father, Ben believed Ten Mile Lake Resort had the kiss of God on it. If there were a place for him to find peace and solitude, it would be on the water's edge. I had to let him be because I knew this was how he needed to grieve in those initial moments.

Jared had gone to bed in his room, and I went in and lay down beside him. I put my arms around him and listened between sobs as he said, "I wish I hadn't seen the accident." I was in agreement with him and began to pray that God would, at that very moment, begin to heal that memory. Being an eyewitness to your father's tragic death was more than a young teenage boy should have to endure, but we served a God who was able to do exceedingly and abundantly beyond all we could ask or imagine. God would use this tragedy to shape Jared's character as a man, not destroy him.

As he struggled to fall asleep, I had my sister make a bed for us on the floor in the family room. Maybe watching TV would be a much-needed distraction. I lay down beside him until the emotional exhaustion of the day finally took over, and he was able to sleep.

I waited for Ben to return home. The concept of time had left me, so I'm not sure how long he was gone, but I was going to be sure I was there for him when he returned. Again, like his father, he was a young man of few words. I did not force him to talk but certainly provided him the opportunity if he needed to. I believe we sat mainly in silence before he made his way to bed. There are times when more is spoken in silence than in words. I believed that was one of those times.

As the morning light was breaking on the horizon, I made my way into Jenna's room and crawled in bed with her. I'm not sure if I woke her or if sleep was impossible. What was filling the mind of my precious little girl was her childhood dream of one day being a bride, and she asked me, "Mom, who is going to walk me down the aisle one day?"

I'm not sure I could have faced a more excruciating question. What do I say to my baby girl who had her own happily-ever-after story playing out in her little-girl dreams?

In the Old Testament, when Abraham was asked by God to sacrifice his son Isaac, Isaac asked his father a very appropriate question. Here is the scene in Genesis 22.

> Abraham took the wood for the burnt offering and placed it on his son Isaac, and he himself carried the fire and the knife. As the two of them went on together, Isaac spoke up and said to his father, "The fire and wood are here but where is the lamb for the burnt offering?" Abraham answered, "God himself will provide the lamb."

I did not have an answer for Jenna but I knew in my heart that God would provide one.

It was now early Sunday morning, and I found myself thinking about my church family and those who would be hearing the news of Pat's death for the first time. We had been a part of our church for twenty-one years. These were people that we did life with: we worshipped with them, we prayed with them, and we fellowshipped in each other's homes. We laughed together and we cried together. I needed to pray for them as much as I needed them to pray for me.

As I left Jenna's bedroom, I knew I had to face the inevitable— going into the bedroom I shared with Pat. I needed to get ready for the day. Pat's sister had arrived by then and accompanied me into the room. I fell on our bed and in my wailing cried out, "Pat is supposed to be here next to me." She gently caressed my hair while I cried and said, "I know, honey." As the tears subsided, I asked her to go in our closet and find me something to wear. I could not yet face seeing his clothes next to mine.

My mind and emotions were not yet ready to deal with funeral preparations that first day after the accident. I needed time to soak in the love and support that was being poured out on us, which there was no shortage of. People took on the role of being the hands and feet of Jesus and surrounded us.

The best way to describe my grief is to liken it to a labor room. Having given birth to three children, I was no stranger to labor pain. A contraction meant the discomfort was going to be excruciating, but it would run its course, and a time of rest followed before the onset of the next contraction.

Throughout the day, as I talked with family and friends, I felt despair rising in the pit of my stomach. I knew I was entering into another time of intense mourning. I literally said "ouch." Loud cries of sadness and heartache were heard throughout our home as I labored through the despair that enveloped me. The room fell silent of conversation but not silent of others weeping with me.

By Sunday evening, I knew God had heard my prayer "help me," and I began to experience His presence in my life unlike I had ever felt before. Psalm 34:18 reads, "The Lord is close to the brokenhearted and saves those who are crushed in spirit." The definition of *crushed* is "to press or squeeze with a force that destroys or deforms."[1]

Despair was pressing in on every side but not to the extent of destroying or deforming me. I was being molded and reshaped by the hands of the Master Potter. He was starting the slow process of piecing together my shattered heart, and it began at the keys of my computer as I planned how my husband was to be remembered.

It was early Monday morning when I made my way into our office to sit before my computer. I was now ready to put in words what was so alive in my heart— the love I had for Patrick Schultz. I know this may sound silly since Pat was not alive to know what I was doing, but I wanted to make my final act of love toward him perfect through his remembrance.

Enveloped in the power and presence of the Holy Spirit, these are the words that flowed from my heart to the paper as I wrote his obituary that morning:

> *Pat Schultz, 44, of Ten Mile Lake, went home to be with his Lord on Saturday, August 20, 2005. He was born November 10, 1960 in Fergus Falls, MN to Jerry and Shirley Schultz.*
>
> *He grew up in the place he treasured most on this earth, Ten Mile Lake Resort. Being the son of a business owner, he started working at a young age by picking up paper around the resort and continued to be*

"promoted" to bigger jobs. In 1991, he and his identical twin brother, Mike, became fourth-generation owners of Ten Mile Lake Resort and Steakhouse.

Pat had the rare privilege of attending country school through the fourth grade. He finished his elementary education at Our Lady of Victory Catholic School and went on to graduate from Fergus Falls High School in 1979. He completed two years at the Fergus Falls Community College, one year at Mankato State University, and one year at Moorhead State University.

On September 22, 1984, he married the absolute love of his life, Lisa Ferber Schultz. Their greatest treasure together was their three children, Benjamin, Jenna, and Jared. The legacy he leaves will forever be lived out in each of them.

Pat cherished his alone time with Lisa and their time together watching and cheering on their children in the many sports they played. He also loved to hunt, play church-league softball, and bowl in the Farmers' league.

Pat loved his Lord and this was clearly demonstrated in his love for his family and extended into his church where he graciously used his spiritual gift of service. He was blessed with family and friends who loved him dearly and who now hold many priceless memories of times spent with him.

Monday afternoon was our scheduled time to meet with the funeral director. There is a lot of planning and preparation in a short amount of time that goes into an unexpected funeral. I was thankful for the help and support of all who sat around the conference table with us that day as decisions were made. I felt forced to be a part of something I wanted no part of, but I also knew everyone else around that table preferred not to be there, either.

I had already made the decision to not have Pat buried with his wedding ring on, but I had not anticipated the feeling of finality I had as the funeral director placed Pat's band in the palm of my hand. As I fell against the wall in despair, I understood in greater depth what it meant to be held by God. Yes, the wall was bracing me, but I needed far more support than a physical structure. While the world around me was once again crumbling, I felt the strong arms of Jesus lifting me.

The most difficult part of that day was picking out the casket. It is a somber moment to walk into a room for the sole purpose of making a purchase that is going to cost hundreds of dollars, and you don't even want what you're buying. The last satin-lined box purchased held a set of rings Pat had placed on my finger. How I longed for that to be the satin box I was looking at once again.

Since Pat had been a woodworker and a rugged outdoorsman, we were drawn to caskets made of solid wood. With every decision, I had Pat in mind and what best reflected him and his life. This was true as I met with the florist, also. As I looked through the various books of arrangements, I knew none of those fit my Pat. There was nothing flowery about him.

He needed something that reflected nature and the environment he loved to spend time in. So I made my way through the floral shop collecting anything and everything an avid hunter saw in the wild. I found cattails, wild grasses, feathers, and branches. With my arms full, I placed all of it on the counter and said, "Please, make an arrangement from this." It turned out perfect. I still have it in my home today.

It was late afternoon when I finally made it back home. I was emotionally spent, but there was still more to do. Pastor Steve and our worship leader came out to plan the services. We planned to have a prayer service and a time of sharing on Wednesday night and the funeral service on Thursday. I had two main objectives: first, that Pat was lovingly remembered, and second, that Jesus was lifted up and His beautiful plan of salvation communicated.

The opportunity to share life in the midst of death cannot be overlooked. A funeral service brings home the finality of life for each of us, which ultimately raises questions about eternity. I was not about to let anyone leave one or both of the services without knowing how they could spend eternity in Heaven where the sting of death touches us no longer.

Another important element to the services was corporate worship. Music has a way of ministering to the soul like nothing else. The Bible instructs us to put on a garment of praise for the spirit of heaviness (Isaiah 61:3 KJV). I was not going to be the only one whose spirit was heavy that day. I wanted, no, I *needed* to worship with those who would be sharing in my sorrow.

On Tuesday, Jenna and I got away, just the two of us, to do some shopping. I was looking for a necklace to wear for the funeral. Pat and I had a longstanding joke between us that whenever I told him I got something new and he asked me how much it cost, I always said $10. Jenna was well aware of this. When I found the necklace I wanted to buy, I looked at the price tag, and it was $10. I showed it to Jen, and we both burst into tears while standing in the middle of the store embracing each other.

To see that price was like a kiss from God on my forehead. Tears were falling from my eyes, but my heart was smiling. I finally bought something that was actually $10. Pat would have been so proud of me! I figured I'd better explain our story to the two young girls working there. I'm sure they had never seen such a reaction to an inexpensive necklace. They struggled to hold back their tears after hearing our story. I know we blessed them that day.

Chapter 7
Grieving With Hope

Each day following Pat's death, I was faced with new challenges that tested my faith and endurance. I woke up Wednesday morning knowing that was the day we'd be viewing his body. I experienced both dread and anticipation, which was a strange mix of emotion. I missed him so much, and I just wanted to see him, but I was so afraid. I had viewed bodies in caskets before, but not my husband's. How would I react?

As I entered the room, I immediately recognized his handsome profile. As I approached the casket, how I longed to have those green eyes looking at me once again. I gently ran my fingers through his thinning dark hair. I felt the chill on his skin. It was a penetrating cold, and it went from my fingers straight through my heart.

I had picked out a pullover for Pat to wear with the Ten Mile Lake Resort and Steakhouse logo embroidered on it, just above his heart. It was there he had lived out his boyhood dreams, and it was there some of his most precious memories were formed. It was there he had brought home his bride and his babies. There was no other place on earth he would want to call home.

I lay my head on his chest, and the mascara wet by my tears stained his pullover. Just one week before, I had wept tears on a warm chest with a beating heart after moving our son to college, and his arms had wrapped around me in comfort. Now, his arms lay folded across his lifeless body, never to hold me again. I begged God to wake him up even though I knew he was more awake than he had ever been in the presence of Jesus.

I had asked my family to allow me time alone with Pat for a while. I mainly did that for my children. I needed to work through my emotions and have my time to fall apart so I could be strong for them.

I also asked Pastor Steve to be there with us. He was the next one to enter the room after me. He hugged me as I sobbed and expressed to him my desire to have just one more night with my husband.

With tears and a broken voice, he entered into my pain and said, "I know. I know."

When I ended my private time with Pat, it was the children's turn to see their dad. Heartbreaking does not even begin to describe what I had to witness. There is a haunting cry that comes from the depths of one's being that is inconsolable, and that is the cry I heard from my babies. It was their daddy's voice that had welcomed them into the world, and his strong arms had carried them. It was his wisdom that had taught them, and his quiet faith had shaped them. All those things were now silenced, and I knew they were longing to hear his voice and to feel his touch once again.

I was there for my children, but I let them express their grief in whatever way it presented itself. They needed to experience the pain of the moment without my attempting to make them feel better. This was a crucial time in their healing journey as they let emotions surface and then were able to release them.

One by one, extended family members made their way to the casket. My heart broke for Pat's mom and dad. We've heard it a thousand times, but the words ring true that no parents should have to bury their child. Though we were grieving together, we individually expressed our pain. Seeing Pat in the casket solidified the reality of the tragedy we were experiencing together. I know each one of us had wished in the previous days that we would wake up to find we were all in the same bad dream. That was not to be. This was life in real time.

As I listened to the grieving of the people I loved most, my heart began anticipating the prayer service that evening. This may sound uniquely strange, but I could not wait to worship the Lord. I had carefully chosen the songs we would be singing, and I longed for the words of those songs to envelop me. I wanted to get lost in their message in the hopes of having some light shine on my darkness. I anticipated the opportunity for the children and me to publicly grieve with hope.

We held the prayer service in the sanctuary of our church because we knew the funeral home would not be able to accommodate the number of people attending. We planned correctly. The line of mourners ran through the sanctuary, into the hallway, and out into the parking lot. I sat on a stool at Pat's head and kept my hand on his shoulder as loved ones passed by the open casket and shared condolences with me. He had been by my side for twenty-one years; I would remain by his for as long as I could.

As 7 p.m. approached, the music started playing, and we made our way to the front row of the sanctuary. One of the songs I had chosen, popular at that time, was entitled, "Draw Me Close to You." The obvious meaning of the words was for God to draw us close to Him, but as we started singing, the words took on a new meaning for me. I got up from my chair, walked to the open casket, and laid my head on Pat's chest, yearning for the chance to be close to him one more time.

It wasn't long until I felt a head resting on my shoulder and an arm around me. It was Benjamin. Jenna and Jared quickly followed his lead, and throughout the remainder of the song, the four of us drew close to each other and close to this one whom we shared a deep love for. It was a moment frozen in time that only those who have experienced such a loss can identify with. The presence of others did not hinder our expression of our grief.

That evening was a time set aside for people to share how Pat had impacted their lives. After so much weeping together, it was refreshing to laugh at some of the memories. I allowed myself to feel every emotion, and laughter was not off-limits. I found delight in the memories we shared.

A common theme was the pleasure Pat received in relentlessly picking on others. He had a mischievous side to him, and if he could irritate you through his pestering or scare you with his untamed, wild side, he was in his happy place.

Many undeniably recognized Pat's servant heart. As I have alluded to, he was a man of few words but not a man of few talents. If there was a need and he could help fill that need, he was on it. Many who spoke had been recipients of his generous heart.

As the time of remembering came to a close, I felt a prompting to share what was in my heart. There were words welling up within me, and like the many tears spilled over in the previous days, these words needed to be spilled out onto the listening ears of those present. I listened to the church's recorded message from that night, and this is in essence what I shared:

> *As I scan this room and see all of you, I am overwhelmed. I asked Jesus this week to allow Pat to look down and see all the love being expressed to us.*

When I came to the church tonight, one of the ladies hugged me and expressed that she felt so bad laying beside her husband last night as she thought of me. I told her not to feel bad but to love her husband and be grateful for the time you have with him. I want to encourage you to show the people in your life that you love them. Don't wait. If there were one thing I could say about Pat it would be that he loved me dearly and he expressed it often. He would tell me that there was no one that could love me the way he did.

On Saturday I was in the ambulance and Pat's breathing changed. It was then I realized my husband was dying. I got out of the ambulance and hit the ground, and I thought I was going to lose my mind. But then I thought of my precious babies, and I received a strength that I can't even explain to you. Jared and our friends came and as we hugged, I said, "The Lord gives and the Lord takes away. Blessed be the name of the Lord."

We went to the funeral home in Park Rapids and the funeral director shared a verse with me from 1 Corinthians 12,"Eye has not seen nor has the ear heard what the Lord has for those who love him." My eye has not yet seen… actually I can't say that because my eyes are seeing each of you, and my ears are hearing how Pat impacted your life. I will not grieve as those who have no hope because I will be with Pat again one day.

The last few days I told myself that I would not allow any thoughts such as I wish or to think about what could have been. I have told my children that Jesus would be lifted up in this tragedy because nothing happens without a reason.

> *You might look at me tonight and ask how I can be so strong, and I look at the tears that have been shed here, and believe me, I have shed many tears. I've shared with many how my grieving is like a labor room, and I wail and wail and then God in His graciousness gives me rest until the next time. I don't know yet what is going to be birthed, but I do know it is going to be beautiful. I just want to thank you. Your presence is a beautiful tribute to my husband.*
>
> *Many of you have known that I love the Lord and that I want my life to always be an example so that others would see Him in me. The greatest tribute you could give to me and to my husband would be if you would love the Lord, too.*

When I finished sharing, Jenna had a poem she wanted to read. Overcome with sorrow, she was unable to speak. Her brothers and I joined her up front. Once again, we supported each other as we stood arm in arm, unified in our suffering. I took the microphone from Jenna and read the words she was unable to utter. It was a poem she had found testifying to the blessing of having someone to call Dad.

***

Thursday morning, the day of the funeral, I filled my home with soothing instrumental music as I prepared for the day. What a weird thing to say. How does one even attempt to prepare? I did all the "normal" things—shower, dress, make-up, and hair. I was consciously aware of what I was getting ready for, but the gravity of this day was most deeply felt when I clasped my $10 necklace.

There were others in my home, but I longed to be alone with God. I needed to once again be kept in the peace that was so much greater than my mind could comprehend. I needed to pray for my precious babies that they too, would be lost in

God's comforting presence. God did not need reminding, but I wanted Him to remember His promise to be a father to the fatherless (Psalm 68:5).

As I walked into the church, I was overwhelmed with a deep sadness as I sensed the magnitude of my loss. I was never again going to walk through those doors with Pat to worship. I was going to see the body that had been home to his spirit and soul for the last time until we were reunited in heaven. I fell into the arms of a dear friend who I know was divinely placed inside the church doors.

Over a thousand people attended Pat's service. There were additional areas set up with close circuit televisions to accommodate the overflow of people. I remember looking in the doorway of one of the overflow rooms as I made my way to the room where family members were gathered. I caught the eyes of fellow mourners, and I was deeply moved by the love and compassion spoken to me through their brief glances.

The family walked into the sanctuary while the worship band led in the song, "I Can Only Imagine." In that moment, all I could do was try to imagine what Pat was experiencing in the presence of Jesus. I better understood the conflict the apostle Paul felt when he said, "I'm torn between two desires: I long to go and be with Christ, which would be far better for me. But for your sakes, it is better that I continue to live" (Philippians 1:23-24 NLT).

My imagination may have taken me to heaven that day while I longed to be with Jesus and Pat and free from my present reality. But once again, the faces of my children reminded me it was better I continued to live.

There was a closeness among Pat's siblings that was truly a rare gift. Each of them had written a letter to Pat that was shared at the funeral. Pat's brother Mike was unable to speak, so his wife Linda stood beside him and read the words he had written to his twin brother:

Dear Pat,

When I look back on our life together, it's hard for me to imagine that you are not going to be there for the second half. I remember all of the fun times we had growing up together, being on the same sporting teams, being called Pat (not Mike) 50% of the time and having conversations with people I didn't even know because they thought they were talking to you. I always let them go on and on and believe that they were talking to you. I remember the earlier years hunting together, playing together, and working together on the resort. I know we didn't always get along and fought with each other, but we always knew we loved each other. It didn't have to be spoken. The connection that only twins have can't be explained to anyone…you just have to be one to know. Thank you for being my brother, my twin. I will not say goodbye but see you later when we will be working together again in heaven as a team with Jesus.

Your Loving Twin,

Mike

Pat was also deeply loved by two older sisters. When the brothers were born, each sister got a brother to hold when their mama needed extra hands. Pat was the smaller of the two babies, so his sister Lisa, who was younger than Sue, was given him to hold. Here are the words she spoke to Pat that day:

My Dear Pat,

For nearly 45 years, you have been in my life. You were the little brother I got to hold for family pictures because we were the smallest. You along with Mike were the little boys who called out at bedtime, "Girls, come kiss us goodnight," only to squirm under your covers making us work for that precious kiss. When we finally found your little faces, we were greeted not by a kiss but a big sloppy lick across our faces.

You were the one who loved to tease me relentlessly. Mike did it too, but you were the instigator. We talked about this not too long ago and naturally you laughed remembering how I broke my favorite hairbrush trying to get back at you. Mom always said you teased me so because you loved me so much. I hope and pray that was true.

I watched with pride as you played football and hockey in high school. I remember leaving college and driving to Fergus to cheer for you and Mike at your games. You probably never knew how proud I was of you, but I was and still am.

I watched you change from a boy to a man when dad needed your help to run the business after our dear Uncle Bob died so many years ago.

I saw how happy you were when you married your Lisa. How you loved her and adored her every day since. On that day she didn't become my sister-in-law rather she became my sister. I love you, Lisa #2.

You and I were blessed with three children each. Some even born in the same years. You were a great dad. Ben, Jenna, and Jared don't ever forget how very much your dad loved you and how much we all love you guys. I got to share our three daughters with you. I got to watch you tease them, too! I always told them in the midst of the teasing, "This is what a brother is like…see what you've missed out on!" They loved you Uncle Pat and always will. Thank you for loving them back.

You will forever be in my memories. I will forever see those mischievous green eyes and you forever and always will have a part of my heart. Love, Lisa

Sister Sue, though six years older, was not exempt from Pat's taunts. Here was her tribute to him:

Dear Pat,

August 20th, the day of your accident, I was in the process of packing our Tahoe. Mallory was moving into her freshman dorm at St. Ben's the next day. Then we received the phone calls that changed our lives forever. First we learned you were in a terrible accident. The next call told us you had died.

Today I am writing you a letter, sharing a few of my memories and thanking you for being part of my life.

I'll never forget my exasperation as a ten-year-old and being asked, "How do you tell them apart?" My response was always the same, "They look different! One is Pat, the other one is Mike! They are not the 'twins'; they are two different people!" It was true. Though you looked identical, you were still your own person.

I remember how you and Mike would not go to bed until Lisa and I would kiss you goodnight. You would call out, "Girls, kiss us goodnight!" We would come into your room and both of you would be hiding under the covers, squirming and giggling, until we gave you a kiss!

Neither you nor Mike could pronounce the letter B. We loved to hear you say, "I have a 'drother'. We share a 'dredroom'." Remember how our cousin Steve called you "Frick and Frack"? Or how it was suggested the two of you shared a brain? I guess that's what happens when you're a twin.

Always the little, irritating brother—I thank you for not letting me forget that I turned 50 in May or that I didn't own a "real" dog. Yes, my dog is an Airedale! Gracie is a real dog!!

Finally, thank you for giving my girls the experience of having a little brother—a lot of love and a lot of good-natured teasing.

Remember our family trip to Florida? How many times did Taylor and Mallory fall for, "What's that on your T-shirt trick?" They still remember. They remember an uncle who could irritate them, take them for fast rides on everything, but always bring them back in one piece. Remember you and Taylor's catamaran spill?

I wish I wasn't writing you a letter to be read at your funeral ... but I am. I promise we will always be here for Lisa, Ben, Jenna, and Jared. I will miss my little brother forever.

Love always, Sue

Pat was adored by seven nieces. This poem was not read at the funeral but was given in tribute from Pat's niece Megan.

Aprons by Megan Deutschman

My uncle had this green apron that he used to wear to work in his restaurant. It was ripped and stained from years of wear, but the green never wore off. The strings were soft from many years of his touch, his hands gently tying them around his waist.

When my uncle was ten, he made my grandmother an apron. It was navy blue with yellow trim and red and blue and green balloons on the front. The apron was my grandma's uniform for thirty-four years.

After my uncle died, my grandma folded her apron and put it in the drawer. She declared she'd never wear it again.

I think those red and blue and green balloons escaped from the pantry; each balloon floating away, doing a little dance through the sky.

Red…blinding pain, circling anger.

Blue…the undisturbed surface of the lake – holding millions of tears.

Green…new and fresh and "Please love the place I left."

Green like my uncle's apron.

Pat's service was a beautiful tribute to a man well loved. I feel incredibly blessed to be able to remember so many details of that day, because I want to remember. Yes, there was a lot of pain, but there was also an overabundance of love. I gave to God that day the million pieces representing my shattered heart to start putting back together, although never to be the same.

When we returned home that evening, the heavens were split, and a rain poured down unlike I had seen in a long time. To me, it was symbolic that the skies above, which served as a canopy over the land where Pat spent his entire life, were weeping. Ten Mile Lake was being filled with tears from heaven.

I don't know if there is anything that can test your faith more than the unexpected and untimely death of a loved one. In her study, *The Patriarchs,* Beth Moore has written, "Somehow we never grow accustomed to the idea that pain and difficulties are part of the human experience. God is not going to exempt His children from life's difficulty. Rather, he highlights those very challenges to prove our faith is genuine."[1]

I know I was being closely watched, as a woman who professed a profound love for her Savior, to see if my faith was genuine. If there were ever an opportunity for me to walk away from God, this tragedy was it. Not for a second was that a temptation.

The summer before Pat died, I had a burden on my heart for family and friends who did not know Jesus as their personal Lord and Savior. I struggled with how to share the gospel message with them in a way that was natural and not forced. When we are healthy and life is good, eternity is not always in the forefront of our minds. An untimely death, however, quickly ushers in that concept.

I don't believe God took Pat to heaven so that I had an opportunity to naturally share the message of salvation, but I was not about to let the opportunity pass by. The Bible tells us in Ecclesiastes 3:11 that God has put eternity in the hearts of all of us. We all have been created with a spiritual thirst and nothing but God can truly satisfy us. Anything apart from Him is only temporary satisfaction.

As I thought about the opportunity before me, I remembered God's promise that He was going to use me one day to help others be free. I always believed I was going to help others find their freedom from mental torment, but the scope of His ministry for me was so much more. Ultimate freedom comes from an intimate relationship with Jesus, and I was given the privilege of proving my faith genuine.

I received this letter shortly after Pat's funeral:

> *Dear Lisa,*
>
> *When I heard you speak at your dear husband's wake, I was inspired to write you and tell you how moved I was by your words. I have never heard such honest heartfelt emotions expressed as you did on Wednesday night; you bared your heart to us. You showed us how very much you loved Pat and how his premature death has affected you and your family. It was also apparent how much Pat adored you and the strong marriage you shared. Thank you for your honesty and letting yourself become vulnerable and sharing the deep emotion in your heart. All of us were touched deeply, more perhaps that you will ever realize.*
>
> *I cannot possibly appreciate the profound loss you are experiencing and will continue to experience. However, I want to tell you how many people's lives have been changed by Pat's death and your expression*

of love for him. I have heard of lives rededicated to Christ, marriages strengthened, sins forgiven, children reconciling with their parents, and numerous people repenting of their sinful ways. And what I have heard is just the tip of the iceberg; I'm sure others have experienced and heard the same. I am absolutely convinced that Pat's tragic death will result in many souls saved to Christ. While this certainly does not ease your sorrow now, perhaps in time it will be a blessing to you. Truly, only God can take a tragedy and bring good from it.

Lisa, so many people are praying for you and your family. I hope that you can feel our prayers. Thank you for being strong and leaning on the Lord in this time of sorrow. You taught each of us how to draw on the strength of the Lord in times of trouble. You also showed us an example of true Christian maturity.

I am going to miss Pat tremendously. Even though I was not a close friend of his, I admired him greatly for his quiet leadership and rock-solid character. He was a man we all depended on and loved as our brother in Christ. He was truly a man of God and a man blessed by God. We will all miss him dearly and carry him in our memories and hearts always.

In Christian love and your brother in Christ, with deep sorrow,

Jim Koenig

PS. When it poured down rain on late Thursday afternoon (wow, what a rain!) I believe the Lord was expressing his own grief and shedding his tears of sorrow for Pat. I always remember how the Lord wept

> *when he visited the grave of Lazarus and saw the people's sorrow over Lazarus's death. Likewise, I believe Jesus wept tears of sorrow for you, your extended family, and the church family, too.*

I did not have a choice in Pat dying, but I did have a choice in how I responded. I had to release him to Jesus, believing there was purpose in his death. If just one person's life was changed by the testimony of our family in the midst of our loss, we had the assurance that his death was not in vain. Jim's letter was our assurance.

Chapter 8
Living a New Normal

Friday morning after the funeral, I knew that many of those who had been with me the day before were returning to life as normal, as it should be. I woke up to face a reality that was my new normal—my happily ever after had died. I was mentally, emotionally, and physically spent, but I still chose to get out of bed that morning and every morning that followed. I was choosing to live and committed to do life the best I could. Three children were counting on me.

Benjamin chose to stay home that fall and not attend college. That was a wise decision. Two major life changes were a lot to walk through simultaneously. We needed to remain close and connected as a family as we embarked on our journey of healing.

Jenna and Jared were attending a private school and classes began the week after Pat's death. The school was so gracious in letting them take as much time as they needed before starting their school year, and even after returning, they were free to come home any time they needed to.

When I was out in public in those first weeks after Pat's death, I remember looking at people who were laughing and thinking to myself, "How can you be so happy? Don't you know what I'm going through?" The reality was they did not know me nor were they aware that my world had been turned upside down. This taught me a valuable lesson. I had often been irritated to see the rudeness and attitude in others; now

I learned to see people with a new set of eyes. Like those who did not know my story, I didn't know theirs, either. I decided that I wanted to treat everyone as though they were in the middle of a crisis and needed someone to understand.

Long-term grief is unpredictable. Days can pass, and in your mind you can think the worst is over, and then without warning, something triggers a memory causing sorrow to burst forth all over again. It was late that fall, and I was mowing the lawn. Thankfully, that was something I always did even when Pat was living. Even if he wanted to mow the lawn, I strongly discouraged it. I was extremely anal about straight lines forming a pattern in the grass. Pat was out to conquer the lawn. That meant crooked lines, diagonal lines, circles, and squares. As much as it irritated me, I would have given anything to watch him recklessly attack our yard one more time.

On this particular evening, I chose to wear a jean jacket I had bought for Pat. It was one he wore often. The breeze created by the back-and-forth motion of our riding lawn mower caused his scent, still lingering in his jacket, to waft through my nose. The floodgates opened, and I began to create a haphazard pattern, like he would have done, as tears blurred my vision. I was feeling so lonely, and I remember crying out to God to fill up my loneliness.

Within minutes, friends unexpectedly began showing up. I returned the lawn mower to the shed, and we built a fire in our pit next to the lake. God began loving me once again through the friends He sent my way. I don't remember the stories we shared around the fire that night, but I will never forget the love that poured out all over me. Whether my friends realized it or not, they had been brought to me in my time of need.

Once the children were settled back at school, and Ben went to work on the resort, I decided to pick up some very part-time employment with a photographer. While getting ready for work one morning, my grief took another unexpected turn. Remember when I spoke at the prayer service and I said that I was not going to allow myself to think, "I wish I would have or if only...?" On this particular day, there was no fighting back those thoughts.

I was agonizing over the things I had said and done that I knew hurt Pat and the things I had never told him I was sorry for. Filled with regret, I cried out to God, "Lord, would you please tell Pat I am sorry for..." and one by one I listed everything that came to mind. I held nothing back. I was in the labor room once again, and the pain was excruciating but necessary.

Do I believe that God went to Patrick in heaven and said, "Lisa is in deep mourning over the things she never said and has asked me to tell you she is sorry"? No, I don't, but I needed to be able to express it for my own emotional health. So many times in my life I had either read or heard it said to keep short accounts with the people you love, and I had not wisely followed that advice, so now I was flooded with memories marked with remorse. To not become paralyzed with regret, I needed to forgive myself.

Often, I thought back to the day of the accident and questioned why the paramedics did not tell me there was a high probability that Pat was not going to make it. I like to believe I would have poured out my heart to him and left no stone unturned. But in the midst of the crisis, would I have even been able to think clearly enough to choose the words I did not want to remain unspoken?

I came across a poem sometime after my day of confession. I know it was not a coincidence because I felt like it was Pat speaking to me from heaven through the pen of David M. Romano:

> When tomorrow starts without me
> And I'm not here to see…
> If the sun should rise and find your eyes
> All filled with tears for me,
>
> I wish so much you wouldn't cry
> The way you did today…
> When thinking of the many things
> We didn't get to say.
>
> I know how much you love me,
> As much as I love you…
> And each time you think of me,
> I know you'll miss me, too.

Pat did know how much I loved him. I was free to let go of the regret.

Going for long drives was therapeutic for me in the weeks following his passing. I knew I could be all alone with no one to bother me so that I could get lost in my thoughts and in my conversations with God. One day while driving, I was thinking about stories I had heard of near-death experiences when people had shared seeing Jesus. It made me wonder when Pat first saw Him. Was it right after he took his last breath, or was it even before that? I decided to ask God.

"Lord, when did Pat first see you?"

In my mind, I heard these words, as clear and audible as if the Lord had been physically present in my car.

"I was with him the entire time. We died a similar death."

Pat's internal injuries were so severe that he basically suffocated as his lungs filled with fluid. Jesus suffocated as He hung on the cross. I believe Patrick was in the presence of Jesus every moment from the time of the accident until he breathed his last breath and the Lord ushered him into glory.

The most common question I heard after his death was, "Why would God take someone so young who had so much life yet to live?"

This is a fair question and one that I wrestled with, also. There are some questions that I deem unanswerable, but then God in His goodness allows us to fall upon a nugget of truth in His word and we can say, "Wow. I think I understand."

I found that nugget of truth in Isaiah 57:1, "The good men perish; the godly die before their time...no one seems to realize that God is taking them away from evil days ahead" (TLB).

I can only guess what may have been evil days for Pat. Had he lived and not been the same man he was prior to the accident, those would have been evil days for him. As I've already said, he was a man of many talents. He used his hands, his feet, his mind, and his strength in his job and in his service to others. I cannot imagine him living without the use of any one of those.

Maybe there would have been an illness, an emotional crisis, a financial loss that would have devastated him. I do not know, and I made the decision to be OK with not knowing. I rest in the fact that God loved Patrick enough to spare him any evil days ahead.

For a while, I allowed myself to entertain a number of "if only" scenarios. If only we would have left home five minutes later. If only we would have been delayed by one more red light. If only the pickup would have been driving slower. You see, the timing of the accident had to be precise for Pat and the truck to meet at the intersection at the exact same time. Friends who visited the accident site after his death said they did not see one vehicle on that road even after staying there for an hour or more.

My "if only thoughts" were silenced by one verse, Psalm 139:16, "You saw me before I was born. Every day of my life was recorded in your book. Every moment was laid out before a single day had passed" (NLT). August 20th, 2005, marked the completion of the days ordained by God for Pat's life. There was nothing that could have been altered to change the outcome.

God had a totally different view of Pat's death than the rest of us. "Precious in the sight of the Lord is the death of His saints" (Ps. 116:15). Now that my children are all gone from home, I think about how excited I get when I know they are coming for a weekend. I carefully pay attention to where they are in their travels so I know exactly when they will show up on my front doorsteps. Likewise, God knows exactly when His saints will be home, and He is there to greet us saying, "I've been waiting for you."

David Romano's poem fittingly concludes:

But when tomorrow starts without me,
Please try to understand…
That Jesus came and called my name
And took me by the hand,
And said my place was ready
In heaven far above…
And that I'd have to leave behind
All those I dearly love.
So when tomorrow starts without me,
Don't think we're far apart…
For every time you think of me,
I'm right here in your heart.

Before Pat's death, I had a speaking ministry. My messages focused on my battles with depression and oppression and how I found my freedom when I learned the true identity of the woman in the mirror. Helping others know and find their freedom in Jesus was a passion that burned within me, and I wondered when I would ever be healed enough to speak again. The opportunity arose in November 2005, just three months after Pat's death.

My Pastor asked if I would speak at church on a Sunday morning. At the time, I did not realize what saying yes to his request would mean for me in terms of healing. That was just the beginning of speaking engagements where I would recount the details of August 20th and the subsequent days that followed.

Saying yes to speaking engagements meant I could not live in denial nor could I get lost in busyness to bypass the pain. Telling the details over and over again forced me to face my reality when I felt like running away. Hearing my own voice speaking the promises of God and confirming where my strength came from were constant reminders that I would be OK.

People could not believe that I was able to speak so quickly and confidently about our tragedy. I, too, marveled at the fact that I was able to talk so candidly about our loss so soon after it had happened. The beauty of the whole experience was that I could say, "It isn't me. It is God working through me." There was no way humanly possible I could do what I did apart from God. For me, choosing to live meant being willing to do what God was asking me to do and trusting that His strength was going to carry me through.

My therapy was looking into the eyes of others who were hurting and sharing my hope with them. It built up my faith, and I knew I would survive.

Psalm 126:5 reads, "Those who sow in tears will reap with songs of joy." I appreciate how my Life Application Bible describes this verse: "God's ability to restore life is beyond our understanding. Forests burn down and are able to grow back. Broken bones heal. Even grief is not a permanent condition."[1] Grief becomes permanent only when we allow it to.

Psalm 23 says, "Yea though I walk through the valley of the shadow of death…" The key word in this verse is "walk"; it is not "sit," "stand," or "set up camp in the valley." We are instructed to *walk through it*. Like in real life, we all walk at a different pace. Depending on whom we are walking with, we often adjust our pace to walk alongside our friend.

One of the most treasured lessons I learned in my grief was how to walk alongside others who are grieving. I don't rush them through the process, but I also don't let them get stuck in one place along the way.

When I feel someone has set up camp in the valley, I've had to gently say, "It is time to move on. You are stuck in the valley."

There are several things that cause us to stay in the valley. The big one for me and for others was regret. It is far too easy to camp out on that one. Instead, we need to acknowledge the areas we regret, seek God's forgiveness, and forgive ourselves. When regrets try to return, take those thoughts captive by remembering they have been taken care of.

We set up camp when we refuse to accept that our loved one is gone. Avoiding activities and people that remind us of our loss is how we choose to cope. Or we go to the other extreme, and we become so preoccupied with the loss that we can't move on. We spend our time longing for the person and the life we no longer have. We will never move out of the valley if we are convinced that life no longer has meaning or purpose.

I believe that in order to keep walking, we have to ask ourselves, what would my loved one want for me? I know Pat would have never wanted his death to steal from us abundant life.

My commentary went on to say, "Our tears can be seeds that will grow into a harvest of joy because God is able to bring good out of tragedy. When burdened by sorrow, know that your time of grief will end and that you will again find joy. We must be patient as we wait. God's great harvest of joy is coming!"[2]

As I continued to speak about Pat's death, my joy began to return. It returned because I was making a difference in the lives of others. I did not sit around licking my wounds and feeling sorry for myself. I am not for a moment trying to underestimate the pain of my journey. It was hard work. There were days when I simply put one foot in front of the other, but I chose to keep walking.

At times, the darkness of despair was so dark that I wondered if I would ever again see the light at the end of this long tunnel of grieving. I read verses such as Isaiah 50:10, "Let him who walks in the dark, who has no light, trust in the name of the Lord and rely on his God." Day after day, I had to make the decision to do just that.

There was a couple who had a seasonal camper on our resort. Diane shared with me that when she couldn't sleep at night, she didn't just lay in bed. She got up and did something. Some nights, she rearranged the pictures on her walls, and to not wake her husband Keith, she took a pair of his socks and placed them over the nail in order to muffle the pounding sound.

One night, she decided to change the furniture around in their family room. When Keith got up the next morning, it was still dark, but he did not turn on a light because he knew his way around the room. Unaware that the furniture had been rearranged, he ran into a chair that had not been there the night before and broke his toe.

As I walked through the darkness trying to maneuver my way through the rearranged furniture in my life, God reminded me that His word was a lamp unto my feet and a light unto my path. He told me to walk in the light while I could, so the darkness would not overtake me, because those who walk in the darkness cannot see where they are going (John 12:35). He reminded me that He came as a light to shine in the dark world, so that all who put their trust in Him will no longer remain in the dark (John 12:46).

Every day, we have choices to make in life. I chose to cling to the word of God when the path of my life took a detour into uncharted territory. The Bible was my road map, and as long as I trusted that it would lead me in the right direction, I could continue to live with purpose.

How I needed that as I embarked on so many changes.

Chapter 9
Change Never Comes Easy

The initial year after the death of a loved one is extremely difficult. It is a year filled with all the "firsts" that you have to endure without the person you love. Our twenty-first anniversary was just one month after Pat's passing. That did not give me a lot of time to adjust to his loss before experiencing the first of my "firsts."

As I thought about how I was going to spend the day, I decided that the only people I wanted to be with were the three children created from the love Pat and I had shared. Pat and I typically went out for dinner on our anniversary, so that is what the children and I did. As I looked into their sweet faces as we sat around the table, I could see their daddy looking back at me. I was so grateful to still have a part of him through them.

Also that fall, in a three-week time period, Pat, Ben, and I all had birthdays. They were quickly followed by Thanksgiving, which led directly into the Christmas season. Whew! I felt I had no time to breathe between special occasions. While facing each of these days head-on was painful, I knew it was an important step toward my healing. Family and friends were there to soften the hurt with their presence.

I continued with a lot of our family traditions but chose to alter others. On birthdays, I still hung the familiar banner and began the day with a lit candle in the center of a cinnamon roll. Family members were invited over for cake and the opening of gifts in the evening. I was not going to let death interfere with the celebration of life.

We often divided Thanksgiving Day by spending time with both sides of our families. Living in close proximity made that possible. We decided, however, that we were going to spend the first Thanksgiving without Pat at his sister's home out of town. It was important for the children and me to be with the Schultz family that day. We all needed to feel Pat's presence in the company of his children.

As we sat around the dinner table with our traditional Thanksgiving feast before us, Pat's sister read a poem she had found. It eloquently spoke of the loss we were all feeling in words we were unable to express. Once again we cried together, fully knowing this was not going to be the last time we were going to shed our tears. Pat's absence was more than obvious. It was the elephant in the room, but we did not ignore it or let it go unaddressed.

Christmas posed an even more difficult challenge for me. As a family, we loved Christmas and our holiday traditions. Typically, we were at my parents' home on Christmas Eve, but that first year without Pat, I did not want to stick to that ritual. I asked my family to come to our home, and we ate pizza while opening gifts. On this particular night, I could not bring myself to sit around a table without him. That first Christmas Eve without Pat, there were many tears that stained our beautifully wrapped packages as we remembered the wonderful gift we had lost.

Christmas Day always began early in the morning with the Schultz family when we opened our gifts after eating breakfast together. That first Christmas, many gifts given to Pat's parents were in memory of Pat. We thought it best to give those presents first, grieve together, and then give ourselves permission to enjoy the other gifts we shared.

After the last package was opened, Pat's mom got out appetizers from the night before, which included her famous shrimp dip. When she brought it out, I started to cry. Pat loved shrimp, but he was allergic to shellfish. He often teased me that if he ever committed suicide, he would do it with a plate of shrimp. I laughed through my tears as I remembered his words.

Birthdays, Thanksgiving, Christmas, and our anniversary were by far the days I dreaded the most, but as I survived each one, it gave me the confidence that I could face future celebrations courageously. I allowed myself to remember, cry, and then be thankful for what I still had.

It's not uncommon for people to work toward creating a place of comfort in life and then wishing nothing would ever change once they got here. Pat and I had reached that point in our life. Then reality hit, reminding me we cannot count on things remaining the same. At any moment, we are susceptible to events that have the capacity to turn our lives upside down, presenting unwanted changes. August 2005 ushered in a year of overwhelming change.

Being in a partnership in a family-owned business, we had set up a buy/sell agreement that came into play upon the death of one of the partners. Mike paid me for our portion of the business and he and his wife became sole owners. The resort was no longer my place of occupation. The stress this caused was not the typical stress caused by job loss. It did not put me in a financial crisis, nor was I faced with the embarrassment of being fired. The stress and heartache came from being separated from a place that was a central part of my life for twenty-one years.

Ten Mile Lake Resort was a community of people I loved and loved to serve. We had a large number of staff working for us and they, too, were very much a part of my life.

Nothing had truly changed in the sense of relationships, and yet I knew nothing would ever be the same. It couldn't be without Pat and without my day-to-day interactions with each of them.

For many months following Pat's death, I had to make myself visit the resort. Thankfully, we had moved off the property three years before the accident so I did not have a constant visual reminder. When I was at the resort, I saw Pat everywhere and in everything, including in his identical twin brother. Both Mike and I were reminders to one another of the great loss we were both experiencing. Even though it was painful, I was overwhelmingly blessed by his protective love for the children and me.

Jenna was entering her senior year of high school when Pat died. There were so many special events that year that served as constant reminders of her daddy's absence. She was an athlete, and we both dreaded parent's night during both volleyball and basketball seasons. Jenna was close to her Uncle Mike and her Uncle Jon, and they both graciously stood in for her father in their support and love.

We could not stop our tears as we stood before the crowd, and it was excruciating to hear my baby girl cry for her daddy. I felt bad for the other senior girls because I did not want our sadness to hinder their special moment with their parents. We were grateful for the support they gave us.

Graduation came far too quickly. One day, I was planting flowers in preparation for Jenna's graduation party. It was one year earlier that Pat and I were doing yard work together before Ben's graduation. Now, bent down in the dirt on my hands and knees, I felt like there was something behind me. I actually turned around and looked, but there was nothing there. Even though I saw nothing, I was overcome with Pat's presence. I believe it was another kiss from God during such a difficult time.

The summer following Pat's death, I began entertaining the idea of moving off the lake and into town. We had a large lot and a large home to take care of, and I wasn't sure I felt up to the task. Church friends had graciously raked our yard that first fall, which was filled with oak trees. I didn't believe anyone was crazy enough to want to do that again. Jenna had plans to leave for college, and Jared and I certainly did not need a home that size.

Since I was no longer employed at the resort, and the majority of our activities took place in town, I did not see any reason to continue living on the lake. It is a decision I later came to regret when I realized how important living there was to Jared. I always knew Ben had a love for everything about the resort life. I did not pick that up from Jared, and so I did not ask him if he was OK with moving. He did fine in town, but I did have some remorse for taking him away from his boyhood home.

Initially, I thought about building a new home. I always heard how much stress building put on a marriage, so I thought it was the perfect time to build while being single. I would have no one to argue with, and I would get the final say in all the planning. Oh, yes. *All the planning*. I became overwhelmed at the thought and started to question if I really wanted the stress in my life at that time.

Fortunately, I found a spec home I loved. There was no guesswork in the final cost, and that gave me peace of mind. I moved out of our lake home by September 1, before the leaves started to fall.

As I settled into our new home, I looked back at the previous year in my life and wondered how I survived it. My firstborn had graduated and moved away from home only to return home after Pat's death and then to leave again after Christmas to start school in the second semester. My husband was tragically killed, and my youngest child witnessed his death.

The life I knew as a business owner on Ten Mile Lake Resort was gone. My daughter went through her senior year without her dad, and I faced her graduation and her leaving home without Pat's shoulder to cry on and his arms to comfort me. I sold our dream home we were only able to enjoy for three years together, and I started life over in a new home in a new location. Only by the grace of God did I survive.

I thought the second year would prove easier, which in some ways it was. I was adjusting to our "new normal," but getting through the birthdays and holidays proved more difficult. The first year, I was anticipating having to face all the firsts. I was somewhat mentally prepared. Then I had to do it all over again the second year; that was when I became truly aware that this was my reality for the rest of my life.

Author and speaker Joyce Meyer has a book entitled, *Do It Afraid*. She says that fear will always try to push us back and is always ready to attack us through our thoughts. We cannot let fear stop us, but rather we have to choose to do it afraid. For the first two years, and more specifically the first several months following Pat's death, it seemed that every day I could exchange the word *fear* with another emotion that I had to fight through.

I had many feelings that would have not only pushed but held me back if I had allowed them to. But I determined that I was going to push ahead and do it alone—heartbroken. I was going to push ahead and do it confused, angry, wanting, and frustrated. I was going to push ahead whether I felt overwhelmed, agitated, anxious, run-down, worn out, or powerless. But overshadowing all the negative emotions, I was going to push ahead and do it trusting, hopeful, and confident because the One who gave me strength had promised to do immeasurably more than I could ask or imagine, according to His power that was at work within me (Ephesians 3:20).

A light was dawning on my horizon.

Chapter 10
Free to Love Again

I always thought I understood loneliness, but not until I was alone after twenty-one years of marriage did I truly feel its sting. As a couple, Pat and I had wonderful friends, and after his death, they loved and cared for me well. My unwanted status of being single did not alienate me from their gatherings.

When Pat was alive, he often worked evenings, and it did not bother me to go to social events solo. If I had to choose between missing out on the fun or going alone, I definitely went alone because I'm all about fun. I never felt strange or out of place because I knew at the end of the day, I was going home to my husband. Sadly, that changed after he died. Immediately, I felt like the third, fifth, or seventh wheel, depending on how many couples I was with. Our friends certainly did not make me feel that way. The reality that I was a widow without a life partner dictated my feelings. I often cried as I drove home, looking at the empty seat next to me.

I will never forget the first New Year's Eve party I went to after Pat's death. When the clock struck midnight, each couple found their mate to share a traditional New Year's kiss. If I had planned things right, it would have been a perfect time for a bathroom break, but avoiding everything painful does not bring healing. *Choosing to live means choosing to endure the things that are difficult*. I knew in my heart that my friends hurt for me as much as I hurt for me.

As days turned into weeks and weeks into months, I felt myself longing for male companionship again. I loved being married and having someone to "do" life with. Being widowed so young, I could not see myself remaining single, but the prospect of dating again produced conflicting emotions. I was both terrified and excited. I wanted to love again, and just maybe there could be a second happily ever after.

It was February 2007 when an online dating commercial came on the TV advertising free sign-up for the weekend preceding Valentine's Day. This certainly was not a holiday I looked forward to after the love of my life had been taken from me, but that commercial opened up an avenue for me to possibly find love again. Once more, I was hit with a barrage of feelings and emotions. Can I really trust an online dating service? What was I potentially opening myself up to?

Pat had been gone only eighteen months, so my initial thought was, "Had enough time passed for another man to be part of my life?" Previously, I had been critical of people who I thought dated too soon after they lost a spouse, so I needed to decide if I was ready for that scrutiny. Ultimately, people have their own timetable, and searching my soul helped me know when the time was right. It was not about whether a certain amount of time had passed, but rather knowing I was dating for the right reasons.

I had been real about Pat's death and had faced it head-on. I was not looking to date to escape my reality because I had taken the time to work through my grief. Pat was not coming back. I would never forget him. I would always love him for the years we shared, for the children we created, and for his part in making me the woman God intended me to be.

I was not trying to find someone to take Pat's place in my life, nor was I looking for another Pat in looks, personality, gifts, or talents. What the two of us had could never be duplicated. I wanted to live in love again, and in doing so, I wanted it to be a whole new chapter, a whole new love that would be uniquely ours. I also knew it would take someone special who could embrace the life of a past love and not be threatened by his memory.

I had made a vow to Pat and even though I knew in that vow I had said, "Till death do us part," I was suddenly feeling guilty for even entertaining the thought of pursuing love again. As I tackled my feelings of guilt, I asked myself, "What would Pat want for me?" I also asked, "What would I want for Pat if I had been the one who died?"

After sharing such a rich love and knowing the blessings of having someone to walk through life with, I knew neither one of us would want the other to go through life alone. Again, my love for Pat did not die when he died, but death had released me from my vows to him, and I was free to love once more. "A wife is bound to her husband as long as he lives. If her husband dies, she is free to marry anyone she wishes, but only if he loves the Lord" (1 Corinthians 7:39).

I was anxious as I thought about how my children would feel about another man in my life. I remembered how I felt after my father passed away from cancer and the first time my mom called to tell me she was going on a date. When I hung up the phone, I started to cry, and I remember telling Pat that I didn't understand why I was crying. I was happy for Mom, but I was struggling as I visualized seeing her with another man. If I were feeling that way as an adult, how would my children process it as teens?

I did not ask them for permission to date, but I also did not hide it from them that I was contemplating signing up on a dating site. I chose to not make a big deal about it.

I thought about Pat's family. I knew it would not be easy for them to see me love someone else, and I was already dreading the thought of having to tell them if, in fact, there was another man in my life. They knew the deep love Pat and I had for one another. We had no problem with public displays of affection, and they often accused us of acting like newlyweds twenty years later. Could I, or even should I, show affection to another man while in their presence?

Despite these concerns whirling about in my brain and the conflicting emotions in my heart, I went ahead and signed up for the free weekend. I felt like a teenager all over again until I looked in the mirror and quickly realized I was a teenager in a forty-three-year-old body. It was best not to think about that!

It obviously had been years since I had dated, so I had no idea what to expect or what a man expected of me. I was thankful for the structure of the dating service guiding me. The initial step in the process was to complete a personal profile. This was quite time consuming but very much worth it. Anyone who took the time to carefully complete it meant they were serious about finding the right partner.

I cautiously chose words that accurately and authentically painted a picture of who I was on the inside. I did include my picture because I do believe that physical attraction plays a role, but what I truly wanted was a man drawn to my inner qualities that could and hopefully would become more beautiful with the passage of time.

After submitting my profile, the dating service looked for potential matches based on submitted profile answers to their questions. Every time I had a match, I received a notification via computer. Each notification was a reminder to me that I was choosing to live, and it felt good. What an eye-opening experience to see and read the stories of the men out there looking for love.

The dating site accomplished what I'm sure they had set out to do, which was to wet my appetite so that when the free weekend was over, I wanted to continue on and pay the price for whatever amount of time I signed up for. There is no way I was going to "kiss" enough toads in one weekend to find another prince charming, so I signed up for a three-month stint.

As matches were generated, I could choose whether or not to accept them, and if accepted by both parties, we continued on with "guided communication" that was designed to help us further discover if we were the right fit for each other. A lot of time was spent getting to know one another online before speaking on the phone or before meeting face-to-face. I appreciated that process.

There were a few men that I never got further with than the online communication. As we answered the guided questions, we concluded there were too many differences to communicate any further. I actually talked to one man on the phone, but it ended up being just that single call. What we saw as potential sparks online never turned into a flame after hearing one another's voice.

One match actually culminated in a date. From that one date, I learned the most valuable lesson that I can share with you: *listen, listen, listen* to the still, small voice that each of us has been blessed with. If there is a prompting that something is not right, then something is not right. I ignored that still, small voice. As I read his texts, I questioned his spiritual and moral character. Some of the things he wrote made me uncomfortable, and when we spoke on the phone, some of the things he said did as well. I felt uneasy inside, but I chalked it up to nerves.

Rather than heeding the promptings I felt inside not to go, I agreed to drive one hundred miles to have dinner with him. Without going into detail, I will just say my still, small voice was correct. He made inappropriate advances that made me very uncomfortable, and I ended the evening early.

I could not stop the tears as I drove home. The next morning, I found myself at Pat's grave where I continued to cry my heart out. It was so hard for me to accept that his body was just a few feet below me, but his arms were never going to hold me again. It was an all-too-familiar posture, lying on the ground, broken, with tears spilling out because of the emptiness I was feeling without him.

More questions arose: Should I continue my search? Is it worth the time and the effort to get to know someone else? I remembered all the adjustments Pat and I had to make after getting married. Did I really want to go through that again? The biggest question I wrestled with was, is it even possible to love someone else while continuing to love Pat?

To each question there was a resounding *yes!* All of the good, the bad, and the ugly that Pat and I went through were so worth it. When my second child was due, I remember thinking, "How will I ever love her as much as I love Ben (my firstborn)?" It proved to be no problem at all. My heart was able to grow in love, and there was always room to love again and again and again. I knew I could love another man.

As I approached the dating site once again, I decided there were three things I was not going to compromise on: first, I would not ignore my still, small voice. Even if I didn't understand why, I would trust that it was for my own good. Second, I would spend ample time communicating through e-mail and phone before ever meeting face-to-face. I did not want any physical attraction interfering with getting to know the heart. And finally, I would not compromise on the qualities a potential mate must have.

He must have a genuine love for the Lord and be committed to serve Him. He must love my children unconditionally and be a father to them without taking the place of their father. And he must be willing to relocate to Fergus Falls. I would not disrupt my children's lives further by uprooting them and moving to a new community.

And then it happened. I was matched with a man, Kevin, from Minot, ND. As I read his profile, I quickly recognized he fit my "must haves." He loved the Lord and God was a central part of his life. Check. He never had children, but he was not opposed to meeting a woman with children. Check, check. He was willing to relocate. Check. Check. Check.

As I carefully studied Kevin's profile, I was attentive to any stirrings I had on the inside, negative or positive. I was not afraid of nor did I hold back from asking him difficult questions. He was genuine and sincere in his answers, and it wasn't long until I was smitten with this man I was learning about via computer. Even though I believed him to be genuine, when he asked for my phone number, I was not ready to give it. We decided that he would give me his number and I would call him when I was ready.

It was a Wednesday morning, on my way to exercise class, when I decided to dial his number. Since it was a weekday, I knew Kevin was at work, so I did not have to worry about him answering. All I wanted at that time was to hear his voice. Wouldn't you know he hadn't personalized his voicemail, so all I got was an automated recording? I disappointedly pressed end on my phone without leaving a message.

After exercise class, I returned to my car, and my cell phone showed that I had a message. When I recognized it as

Kevin's number, my heart started racing. Not knowing for sure if it was me or one of his shippers, he left this message, "Hi, this is Kevin with SpeeDee Delivery. I'm sorry I missed your call." I got what I wanted. I heard his voice. Pleasant to the ears, I might add! Now what do I do?

I nervously decided to call back. This time he answered. Because he was working, we talked briefly and he asked if it would be OK to call me that evening. After a quick internal check of my still, small voice, I enthusiastically agreed to his call.

For the next six weeks, Kevin and I had a phone date every evening. I had a chair in my bedroom that I would curl up in and listen to the man whose voice I longed to hear. With both of us being in our midforties, there was so much to talk about. There had been many years of experiences and relationships that had impacted and shaped our lives. There were times when the rose-colored glasses came off, and we allowed ourselves to be vulnerable with one another about the tough times in our past.

Kevin was no stranger to a sudden death, having lost a brother in a tragic car accident. Even though it was not a spouse, I knew we both understood the sting of death. He also had dealt with the personal loss of a failed marriage. Having discovered you cannot "fix" another person broke his heart and resulted in the death of his happily ever after. We were both in search of it once again.

My favorite things to talk about with Kevin were my children. Each one was so beautifully unique, and I had the privilege of telling him about their personalities, interests, hobbies, and so on. He enthusiastically listened and asked questions to learn more about them. I knew he wasn't pretending to care when each evening as we ended our conversation in prayer, he took time to pray for each of them by name. Listening to him pray, I heard an intimacy with the Lord that could not be manufactured, and that quality more than anything captured my heart.

Kevin could not in return share enthusiastic stories about his children since he and his ex-wife were unable to conceive. As difficult as it was not to be a father, he understood the Lord's providence in sparing children from the dysfunction that had plagued his marriage.

After six weeks of long-distance conversation, we decided we were ready to meet face-to-face. June 1, 2007 was the date we set. Kevin had a full day of work before his five-hour drive to Fergus Falls. Being a difficult city to navigate, I made arrangements to meet him at a convenience station just off the interstate. Not the most romantic setting for a first encounter, but that was quickly improved upon when he stepped out of his truck with a beautiful bouquet of a dozen red roses nestled in greens and baby's breath.

He was more handsome in person than his pictures on line portrayed. Even though we had not yet realized it, Kevin and I had fallen in love over the phone, which made giving each other a hug seem natural and not the least bit uncomfortable. I wondered if he was feeling the same rush of emotion that I was. It felt good to feel that way again.

My sister was not at home for the weekend, so she offered her home for Kevin to stay in. It was late by the time we got over there, but we still settled in for an even later night of conversation. It was about to be revealed if the Kevin on line was the same Kevin in person. Without a doubt, he was.

My son Jared was at a friend's who lived across the street from my sister. He came over to meet Kevin, and they hit it off immediately. It was not difficult to see that Kevin was genuinely interested in my son. They shared a love for sports, so once the conversation went in that direction, I couldn't get another word in. That was perfectly fine. I enjoyed being a spectator to their interaction.

After Pat died, there were men in our church who stepped up and watched out for my children and me. I knew they would come to my rescue if I needed anything. But it wasn't until I met Kevin that I saw how they were also there to protect me.

My pastor asked if he could come with me when I met Kevin for the first time. He said he would be wearing a gun and holster, and he would let him know that if he messed with me, he would be messing with the entire church. Even though he was funny in getting his point across, I knew he was serious about his protectiveness and the protectiveness of the rest of my church family.

On Saturday, Kevin and I were at a coffee shop when I received a phone call from another man at our church asking me if everything was going OK and if Kevin was treating me well. He assured me that he was only a phone call away if I needed anything. I was blown away by these gestures of love.

Kevin was amazing in his interactions with so many different people that weekend. I marveled at how well he remembered names. When he wasn't in earshot, my friends were whispering their approval, which meant more to me than they will ever know, because I trusted and valued their judgment. I was excited to introduce him to Mom because she was the one I showed his pictures to and said, "Doesn't he look sweet, Mom?" I knew she would enthusiastically share in my joy, and she did.

Because our weekend went so well, and we quickly realized this was not a one-and-done relationship, I decided to travel back to Minot with Kevin to meet his parents. I know, you are saying, "You are kidding right?" But I'm not. It was going that well.

Kevin had an apartment in the basement of his parents' home, which made it convenient for me to get to know them while he worked during the day. I was just as comfortable with Kevin's parents as I was with him. I quickly learned where he received his gentle spirit and kind heart. I discovered the rich, godly heritage in which he was raised, not just in his parents but it was also very evident throughout his extended family.

Kevin's mom had struggled with him dating again after his divorce, but she had given it over to God just before he met me. She prayed that if it was right for him to marry again, he would find the right woman. Within days, we were matched on the dating site. God was answering her prayer.

I stayed in Minot for a few days, and then Kevin and I met Jenna halfway so I could get back home again. As Kevin and I talked while driving, he shared with me that even though we had only known each other briefly, he knew in his heart he wanted to marry me. Strangely enough, that did not freak me out. On the other hand, he made the mistake of telling that to my daughter and that definitely freaked her out.

This began a very rocky time in my relationship with Jenna. She was completely up-front with me in saying she did not appreciate his statement and that she also did not want to share me with anyone. Jenna and I had always been so close, but for the next several months, any time I talked about Kevin, she immediately put up a wall of defense. Jenna does not hide her emotions well. Her body language spoke volumes to me, and I struggled to know the right thing to do.

For several months, Kevin made the ten-hour drive each weekend to visit me. We grew more and more in love, and marriage was definitely a part of our future plans. As I searched my heart, I decided that the child I needed most to talk with about my remarrying was Jared. He was the one who would still be living at home for the next three years and be most directly affected by my marriage to Kevin.

Ben was established in his own home and working on the resort that we had owned. Although Jenna disapproved of my involvement with Kevin, at nineteen years old, she was away at college setting the course for her own adult life. Jared, on the other hand, was a sophomore in high school and would be the one sharing a home with a man who was not his father. I took him out for dinner one evening and asked him how he felt if I married Kevin. I let him know that I loved him and would respect his wishes. He did not hesitate to give me his approval.

On September 16, 2007, Kevin gave me a ring. That was a day that had been marked by sorrow for me after losing my dad on that date in 2002 but would now from this time forward mark a much happier occasion. My engagement to Kevin was so similar to how it happened with Pat and me.

I accompanied Kevin to the jewelry store in Minot where we picked out my ring together. The setting I chose was available in three different-sized diamonds. I told Kevin that I did not need the largest one, size was not important to me, but he generously gave to me what I did not ask for. It would've been difficult to turn that down, right ladies? So I didn't.

Once again, I did not wear the ring out of the store. I would be lying to you if I said I was not experiencing any fear or second thoughts as we walked back to the car. I even said to Kevin, "Are you able to get your money back if anything should happen?" I can't believe I asked that because in essence I was saying, "Just in case I change my mind." Were these feelings natural? Why does getting engaged at forty-four feel so different than it did at twenty?

That evening, alone in Kevin's apartment, he shared with me all of the reasons why he loved me and wanted to spend his life with me. His words calmed my fears and gave me the confidence that this was God's plan for us.

I said to Kevin, "This would be the perfect time for you to give me my ring."

What he had said to me was so beautiful, I knew then I did not have to be assured by the passionate and somewhat immature love of a young twenty-year-old—not that there is anything wrong with that. In your forties, however, it is just different. You are more interested in learning about each other. What concerned you in your twenties is replaced by a love that is deeper and truer. Pat and I grew into that love over time together. Kevin and I started there. Because of our life experiences, we knew there was no need to be superficial but to focus on what is important in both love and life. This was a mature love.

As I drove home from Minot, I kept my left hand positioned on the steering wheel where I could watch my ring sparkle in the sunshine. As excited as I was anticipating my future with Kevin, I was equally anxious about sharing the news with Pat's family and with Jenna. Even though I knew it would not be easy, I believed that it would all work out.

As anticipated, it was not easy for them to adjust to the idea of my marriage, but they also did not hold me back. I included Jenna as much as possible in the wedding preparations. Jenna and her brothers were our wedding party, so I enjoyed the time we had together shopping for wedding clothes. Ironically, she was working at a suit and tuxedo shop at the time and was instrumental in getting suits for Kevin, Ben, and Jared. Despite being actively included in the preparations, it was a slow journey of acceptance for my baby girl.

We were married on December 29, 2007 eight months after being perfectly matched on a dating site. We had a fairly large wedding with over two hundred invited guests. Pastor Steve did a beautiful job of bringing Pat into the ceremony. He did not avoid the elephant in the room but rather communicated how pleased Pat would be to know that Kevin was going to be taking care of me.

People who loved us and genuinely desired our happiness surrounded us. People who had walked my journey of grief and shed tears with me were now walking my journey of joy and shedding tears of a different kind…happy tears. I'm not sure Jenna's tears nor those of the Schultz family had made the switch, but in my heart, I knew the day of complete acceptance would come.

After sharing a meal with our invited guests, Kevin and I said our good-byes as we left for a minihoneymoon. With the busyness of wedding preparations and moving Kevin to Fergus Falls, I had not allowed myself to work through the emotions of our wedding night. But God had placed a man in my life who was not threatened by the love of another man.

He understood and tenderly held me on our wedding night as I cried over feelings of unfaithfulness. I believe it was Kevin's understanding and his gentleness that brought me to a place of complete healing and surrender where I could lay those feelings to rest. I was not breaking a previous marriage vow. I was entering into a new one, and my commitment was now to Kevin.

The start of a new year also marked the start of a new life. Kevin actually had far more to adjust to than I did. He was born and raised in Minot, and it had been his home for forty-six years. Everything that he called familiar was now over three hundred miles away. SpeeDee Delivery transferred him to their branch in Fergus Falls, but he still had a whole new route to learn in completely unfamiliar territory.

In addition, he was now a stepfather. What would, or better yet, what should this role look like? He assured my children that he was there for them but that he would never try to take the place of their father. Kevin wanted to be loved and accepted by my children without forcing a relationship. It was a time of adjustment for all of us, and I knew time would be our most valuable asset.

We were in the heart of Jared's basketball season, and it was so much fun to watch Kevin's enthusiasm as he cheered on the team and Jared in particular. And of course, once we got home, they had to relive the game in their conversation. Because Jared was living with us, it was easier for him and Kevin to connect. We had to be more intentional to develop his relationship with Ben and Jenna.

Kevin and Ben shared a love for hunting. This was a special thing Ben had always done with his dad, and eventually it would become a shared experience for him and Kevin as well. So much about relationships is built around the things we have in common, and this was definitely true in making a meaningful connection between Kevin and the boys.

Kevin built a relationship with Jenna by being there for her. He helped move her to Minneapolis, and when she transferred schools, he helped move her to Kansas City. He showed genuine interest in Jenna's life and often called her to see how she was doing. He never pushed but rather let any bonding that was to take place happen naturally.

I did not intentionally compare Kevin with Pat; it just happened in the day-to-day activities of life. It wasn't a bad thing. It just revealed to me that I married two very different men in terms of abilities and priorities, but two very similar men in terms of unconditional love and affection toward me.

Pat was a jack-of-all-trades who could fix just about anything and never let me hire someone to do a job that he could do. Ultimately, this left many things undone because he never found time to get around to doing them. As my brother-in–law says, "Pat was an 80/20 guy." He enthusiastically started a project, completing 80 percent while the remaining 20 percent never got done.

Kevin is much like my father was—there are some small jobs he will venture to tackle but he is not necessarily a handyman. He recognizes the things he can't do, so he doesn't have a problem hiring someone who knows how to do them.

Whenever I used Pat's vehicle, I wasn't sure what I would find under the pile of papers, tools, and wrappers. I was afraid I'd have an asthma attack (which I actually don't suffer from) as the vents stirred up the dust on the dashboard. Kevin, again, kept his truck the same way my father did. He always cleaned it out as soon as he got home. There were no surprises to be found.

Patrick's motto in life was throw caution to the wind—the faster the better. Kevin, on the other hand, thinks of everything that could possibly go wrong and doesn't hold back in telling me what they are. He is definitely not a risk taker.

As different as they were in many areas, they were very much alike in the tenderness of their hearts. I've had the blessing of being completely loved by two men. Some never find that type of love even once during their lifetime, and I've received this gift twice. My gratitude overflows.

God knew I had a lot to learn from these two men. I can be a very stubborn German and I'm quite skilled in the silent treatment when I'm not happy. I'm not quick to give affection if I'm irritated, but I've been given husbands who love me through all my ugliness, and God has said, "Watch carefully and learn."

The greatest fear I had entering into marriage with Kevin was how we were going to essentially mesh four families: our immediate families, my birth family, the Schultz family, and the Freds. For over two decades, we knew how we were going to spend holidays and birthdays. What adjustments were we going to have to make? Did I have to choose between Kevin and the children when it came to deciding where to spend the holidays, in particular, the holidays with the Schultzes?

It did not take long, however, for Pat's family to love and accept not only Kevin but his parents, too. They were immediately assimilated into our traditions. We still spent Christmas Eve with my side of the family and Christmas Day with the Schultzes. Birthdays, Fourth of July, Thanksgiving, and Easter were spent in combined celebration.

I will be forever grateful to Kevin and his parents for sacrificing their traditions to become a part of ours. I will be forever grateful to my family and to the Schultz family for welcoming Kevin and his parents into their homes, but more importantly, into their lives.

Several years have now passed since Kevin and I said, "I do." Weddings have taken place, and grandchildren have been born. Each event has been bittersweet as we remember Pat in the midst of our celebrations. I cannot tell you the number of times Kevin shed tears while saying, "Pat should be here, not me." I've never questioned his thankfulness for being a part of our family. It is a display of the goodness of his heart.

When Pat died, Jesus became my husband and defender (Psalm 68:5). I've had to ask myself, "If I had never found love again, would Jesus have been enough?" I believe I can say, yes, but at the same time, I'm so glad he saw fit to give me Kevin.

Love the second time around is a beautiful thing.

Chapter 11
Helping Our Children to "Suffer Strong"

The children and I certainly did not ask to be thrown into a season of suffering, but then nobody ever asks for that. We live in a fallen world, and therefore adversity is unavoidable. It is one thing for us to suffer, but heaven forbid should our child have to suffer. In fact, we go to great lengths to protect and shield them from it. From the time they are born, we immediately attend to their cries to alleviate hunger, a wet diaper, or a gassy tummy.

When they go in for their well-baby shots, we shed tears as they cry out with the needle poke. As they grow and learn to walk, we remove or cover any obstacles that they could fall against and get hurt. We carefully strap them in their car seats even if we are only traveling a short distance. As they start to play with other children, we are there to protect them from the neighborhood bully. We set up curfews and monitor friends because we have it in our hearts to shield them from harm.

But even though we go to great lengths to protect them, pain and adversity will eventually be a part of their lives; they are unavoidable. So one of the greatest gifts we can give our children is to help them to "suffer strong." How they learn to handle suffering will make or break them in life.

I had not intentionally done anything to prepare my children to suffer strong, and then we were thrust into this fiery trial together. I knew they would be watching me to see what I still believed about God and how I was going to walk through this unwelcomed journey. *Huge* responsibility. The challenge for me was great as I worked through my own grief while trying to shoulder the burden of my children's pain. I hurt for them, and I desperately wanted to make their pain go away.

I was very thankful that the Lord was the center of our home the night that Pat died. My children knew the love and strength of Jesus, so I could confidently point them to Him as the One who would lead us in the darkness.

In the initial moments and days after Pat's death, the one thing I did not do was try to fix our situation with the right words. There was no fix. I could honestly say to them, "I don't know why your daddy had to die." But I knew I could not say, "Everything will be OK," even if I believed it in my heart. When the pain is so fresh and real, a child does not comprehend, "Everything will be OK." How can life ever be OK without their daddy?

I had to listen to their questions and answer them as truthfully as I could. For example, one night after Pat had died, Jenna and I were lying in bed together, and she asked me, "With so many evil people in the world, why would God take Dad?" Jenna wanted an answer to that question.

To the best of my ability, I explained to Jenna that unfortunately bad things do happen to good people. I went on to say, "God does not wish anyone should die without knowing Jesus as their Savior, so if an 'evil' person, or any person for that matter, had died without having a personal relationship with Jesus, they would spend eternity in hell. Your daddy was ready to meet Him because he had a relationship with him. We want that same opportunity for everyone."

As much as I knew there were no words to fix our situation, I did know that the words of Jesus could bring comfort, so whenever I could, I pointed them to the scriptures that spoke of the hope we have in Him. It was a proud moment for me when my oldest son shared at the prayer service. He said it wasn't easy to know what to say, but it meant a lot to have everyone's support.

He ended by saying, "Dad, I love you, and I will miss you, but it is not good-bye because I will see you again."

He was already anticipating that glorious reunion he would have with his dad in heaven because he believed in that promise found in the word of God.

Death brings unasked for and unwanted role changes. As a young man and my firstborn, Ben naturally took on a leadership role in our family. It is heartwarming to look back and remember how Jenna and Jared very naturally followed his lead during our time of grieving. It was the darkest time in the lives of my children, and as their mom, I could not have been more proud.

In John 16:33, Jesus spoke these words: "I have told you all this so that you may have peace in me. Here on earth you will have many trials and sorrows. But take heart because I have overcome the world" (NLT). When Jesus died on the cross, the power of evil that Satan brought to earth was defeated. Included in this was the power of death. Jesus made sure death would not have the final say. That is why I could trust God and experience His peace as I walked my mourning journey, and I longed for my children to also experience God's peace as they walked theirs.

I did not at any time want to communicate to my children that life was going to be easy, but I did want them to know this path of suffering we were on was a temporary journey of intense pain resulting in a life that would never again be the same. Peace is never about the absence of difficulty. Peace for us was in Christ and Christ alone.

My intimacy with Jesus lived out before my children demonstrated that I believed Christ had not abandoned us in our time of sorrow. We were not alone. We could claim His peace because even when life is bad, God is good, and we can have the peace that the Bible describes as "beyond our understanding" (Philippians 4:7).

I needed to communicate to my children about the radical love of God, a love that will never let go. I was in a stage of life where I was learning to let go of them so they could become the people God wanted them to be. Our children are not ours to keep. We have them in our possession for a few short years. What we teach and model in those years is crucial. But equally important is how we handle giving them their independence.

Even though it tore at my heartstrings when I moved my children to college, I could let them go because I knew that God would never let go. He loves us like infants our whole lives. We never outgrow our need for Him. Even as I worked to raise children who would be independent of me, I never wanted them to be independent of God. In the midst of our tragedy, nothing could be more important than their complete dependence on their Heavenly Father.

Deuteronomy 4:9 says, "Only be careful, and watch yourselves closely so that you do not forget the things your eyes have seen or let them slip from your heart as long as you live. Teach them to your children and to their children after them." If there was ever a time I needed to be careful to not forget how God had carried me in the past, this was the time. This was also a time of testing to see how well Pat and I had done teaching our children about the protective, sustaining hand of God.

From the time we are children and throughout our adult lives, we often complain that life is not fair. How true this is. It's not fair when you've studied hard but still fail the exam; when you've practiced as hard as a teammate yet sit on the bench; when you are a dedicated employee and don't receive a promotion; or when a child, with his or her whole life ahead, dies from cancer; or when you lose your father in a tragic accident. When life isn't fair, it is important that our children know God is still sovereign.

What exactly does this mean? The sovereignty of God is the biblical teaching that all things are under God's rule and control and nothing happens without His direction or permission. We have to strongly communicate to our children that nothing happens in their lives unless God has allowed it to happen. That can seem real cruel to hurting children, but we still need to encourage them with the truth that God will use even the most tragic circumstances to fulfill the plans He has for their lives.

Romans 8:28 assures us, "In all things God works for the good of those who love him, who have been called according to his purpose." God had called my children and me, and we responded to His call by loving Him with our whole hearts. Because of this, we could claim the promise of this verse. It didn't mean God would change the outcome of August 20, 2005. It didn't mean God was calling the accident "good."

What it did mean was that one day our eyes would see, our ears would hear, and our minds would comprehend what God had planned for my children and me—just as the funeral director had divinely spoken. These were the promises I had to encourage them with. Light would once again shine in their darkness. I wanted them to learn to accept and not resent pain and suffering because God would always be with them and positive things would emerge from their pain.

So what did I do to help my children suffer strong? I did my best to model suffering before them. I did not hide my tears and my anguish. I cried out to God as I labored in grief so that they could see me run to the One who I knew held the answers. If I could be honest before God as I cried out to Him, then they could know that they could be honest with God about their pain, too.

In Hebrews 5:7-8 (TLB), we are told that Jesus Himself honestly and openly cried out to His Father, "Yet while Christ was here on earth he pleaded with God, praying with tears and agony of soul to the only one who would save him from premature death. And God heard his prayers because of his strong desire to obey God at all times. And even though Jesus was God's Son, he had to learn from experience what it was like to obey when obeying meant suffering."

I not only talked with God, I did my best to openly talk with others about the pain I was feeling so that my children could see the importance of talking through the pain. Of course, I wanted my children to communicate with me, which they did, but I also wanted them to know it was perfectly OK to confide in a trusted friend or another adult who was there to listen and share wisdom. If they'd needed additional grief counseling with a professional, I would have been the first to make that happen.

"A trusted friend" is really a key phrase. In dealing with their discomfort, my children did not always make wise and godly decisions. I do not fault the friends they were with because ultimately my children are responsible for their own behavior. The response to bad choices was, "I just wanted to feel better." As much as I understood that, I did not let them off the hook from the ensuing consequences. I did not allow their grief to be an acceptable reason for making bad choices.

But it gave me the opportunity to say and to demonstrate that I loved them unconditionally.

Looking back, did I do everything right? Absolutely not. I relied a lot on observing my children, and if it "looked" like they were doing OK, then I was OK. I've played the role of an ostrich more than once by burying my head in the sand and living in a state of "ignorance is bliss." Even though my children came out relatively unscathed, I could have done a much better job helping them identify where they were hurting.

I wish I had asked them more questions during the grieving period.

"How are you doing?"

"Are you sleeping through the night?"

"What are you missing most about your dad?"

"Are you angry at God?"

"Do you have any regrets about things you should have said to your dad but didn't?"

"What brings you comfort right now?"

I missed opportunities of ministering to them, and I have graciously welcomed their feedback on what I could have done better.

Living in America has not done justice to the term *long-suffering*. We live in a time when if we want something, we want it now. We are irritated if we have to wait for our fast food and our hunger can't be immediately satisfied. A slow-responding computer causes us to smash the keyboard with our fist (yes, I've done that) when the information we are looking for is not readily available. When a headache strikes, there better be medication in the cupboard so life is not interrupted.

There is no quick fix to suffering. Our initial response may be to shield our children from it, but a greater response is to pray that they would grow into the person God created them to be as a result of the pain.

In death, things will never be the same.

People are never the same.

Chapter 12
Why I Chose Jesus

A man was out for a walk one day when he heard a pack of dogs fiercely barking. At first, the sound was in the distance, but it kept getting closer. It wasn't long until this man saw several dogs chasing a young deer out of the woods and through a field. Intrigued and obviously concerned about the deer's welfare, the man stood next to a fence to watch and see what was to unfold. By this time, the deer's energy was about spent, and a look of terror filled its eyes. But the dogs were relentless. Suddenly, the deer saw the man as he stood by the fence. Wearily, he made his way over to him, and the deer buried its head into the man's chest. The man had become a sanctuary for the tired deer.

Whom do you run to when you are going through times of suffering? Are you comfortable with any listening ear, or do you reach out to someone who has experienced similar pain? The person who says, "I feel bad for you, but I can't relate," is typically not the one we want beside us. No, it is the one who says, "I've been where you are, and I understand. I will walk this journey with you."

Not long after Pat died, I attended a conference in Charlotte, North Carolina. I was riding in the elevator and struck up a conversation with the lady riding with me. We discovered in that short amount of time that we had both lost our husbands at a young age. When the elevator stopped on the main floor, the doors opened to another woman waiting to enter. The lady whom I just met put her arm around me and said to the woman waiting, "She is one of us." These were five of the most powerful words spoken to me after Pat's death. I knew they understood.

Suffering makes us feel exposed. We are out there in the open for all to see, and believe me, people are watching. Suffering also makes us feel vulnerable, and in our helpless state, we desperately search for someone who understands. Looking back on my life, there is only One who has understood every trial, every heartache, every form of hurt, and every emotion I could possibly feel. His name is Jesus, and He identifies with each of us because he was "a man of sorrows and familiar with suffering" (Isaiah 53:3).

Jesus made a deliberate choice to identify with us by entering into our world and living as a human. He faced the same things that we face day after day. He spent thirty-three years on earth—a relatively brief amount of time—but He spent that time loving, teaching, delivering, and healing His followers. He spent thirty-three years experiencing life up close and personal in order to be a Compassionate High Priest who can sympathize with our weaknesses.

I want to take you on a journey through scripture to silence any doubts of whether or not Jesus understands.

- He suffered discouragement. When the disciples could not drive out the demon that was seizing a young child, we hear Christ's discouragement in his response, "O unbelieving and perverse generation. How long shall I stay with you and put up with you?" (Luke 9:41)
- He felt anger. "Jesus entered the temple area and drove out all who were buying and selling there. He overturned the tables of the moneychangers and the benches of those selling doves. 'It is written,' he said to them, 'My house will be called

a house of prayer, but you are making it a den of robbers'" (Matthew 21:12-13).

- He experienced hunger. "After fasting forty days and forty nights, he was hungry" (Matthew 4:2). Quite the understatement!
- He got tired. "Jesus was tired from the long walk in the hot sun and sat wearily beside the well" (John 4:6 TLB).
- He was tempted. "Then Jesus was led by the Spirit into the desert to be tempted by the devil" (Matthew 4:1). "For we do not have a high priest who is unable to sympathize with our weaknesses, but we have one who has been tempted in every way, just as we are—yet was without sin" (Hebrews 4:15).
- He suffered betrayal. "Now Judas, who betrayed him…" (John 18:2). Judas led the captors to Jesus as He prayed in the Garden of Gethsemane.
- He suffered grief over the death of someone he loved. "When Mary reached the place where Jesus was and saw him, she fell at his feet and said, 'Lord, if you had been here, my brother would not have died.' When Jesus saw her weeping, and the Jews who had come along with her also weeping, he was deeply moved in spirit and troubled. 'Where have you laid him?' he asked. 'Come and see, Lord,' they replied. Jesus wept. Then the Jews said, "See how he loved him!'" (John 11:32-36)
- He experienced sorrow. "As he approached Jerusalem and saw the city, he wept over it" (Luke 19:41). Jesus was foreseeing the judgment that would fall upon the nation of Israel because

of their rejection of Him and it filled him with great sadness.

- He was the object of ridicule. "Those who passed by hurled insults at him, shaking their heads and saying, 'You who are going to destroy the temple and build it in three days, save yourself! Come down from the cross, if you are the Son of God!' In the same way the chief priests, the teachers of the law and the elders mocked him" (Matthew 27: 39-40).

- He suffered physical pain. "Nobody performed an autopsy on Jesus's mangled body after He was taken down from the cross. But doctors who have studied the Bible's description of His death say the pain would have been beyond excruciating. In fact, the word *excruciating* means "out of the cross." Jesus literally defined the worst pain anyone could feel.

  After His arrest, Jesus was flogged so mercilessly that his skin was stripped off His back, exposing muscle and bone. After being slapped, punched, crowned with thorns, and beaten with reeds, He was covered with a red robe and led to Golgotha. There, Roman soldiers drove seven-inch nails into his wrists (most likely hitting the median nerve, causing more blinding pain), and then they rammed another nail into his feet.

  At that point, doctors suggest, Jesus would have suffered dislocation of His shoulders, cramps, and spasms, dehydration from severe blood loss, fluid in His lungs, and eventual lung collapse and heart failure. Yet, He refused to take a painkilling solution (see Matthew 27:34).[1] The physical beatings were so intense that Isaiah 52:14 tells us, "...his appearance was disfigured beyond that of any man and his form marred beyond human likeness."

- He experienced abandonment by his Father. Matthew 27:45-46 describes for us the darkest hour in the life of our Savior. For the first and only time in all of eternity, Jesus was separated from the Father. Deeply afflicted, Jesus cried out, "My God, my God, why have you forsaken me?" (VS. 46). It was during this hour he was left completely alone while he took upon himself the sins of the world. There was no one he could call on to deliver him or to comfort him. Even his Father had to abandon him because a righteous God cannot look upon sin. The period of spiritual separation from his Father produced great agony.

Based on what we just read in scripture, we can see that Jesus understands our suffering and has compassion for what we are going through. This is why I chose Jesus and why I continue to choose Him every day. He sympathizes with me by suffering alongside me. Isaiah 63:9 says, "In all their affliction, He was afflicted and the Angel of His Presence saved them…" John McArthur, in his *Study Bible*, explains this verse by saying, "The Lord Jesus Himself is sometimes identified as the Angel of the Lord. He was close enough to His people that He felt their afflictions as if they were His own."[2]

He knows that the struggles of life are too much for us to bear alone so He lovingly assures us with these words, "Fear not, for I have redeemed you; I have summoned you by name; you are mine. When you pass through the waters, I will be with you; and when you pass through the rivers, they will not sweep over you. When you walk through the fire, you will not be burned; the flames will not set you ablaze. For I am the

Lord, your God, The Holy One of Israel, your Savior" (Isaiah 43:1-3).

As I read this promise again, I thought of my Pat, remembering the agony in which he died, but feeling comforted by the Lord's words. I said it before; Pat was not alone while he passed from this life into the next. Hebrews 2:10 tells us that Jesus suffered death so that by the grace of God, He might taste death for everyone. Jesus led the way into heaven as our forerunner. There was no one more qualified to pass through the waters and walk through the fire with Pat on his way to eternity.

In our limited comprehension on this side of heaven, it can be difficult to understand exactly what it means for the Lord to walk with us. You might ask, "How do I know He is beside me when I cannot see or touch Him?" This is where faith comes in. "Now faith is being sure of what we hope for and certain of what we do not see" (Hebrews 11:1).

When we walk with God, we are all given a measure of faith that is not based on what we see. God has given us the gift of divine assurance, which allows us to believe that He will do what He says He will do. Sometimes, we are given a feeling of peace in the middle of the storm where we just know He is with us. Other times, we are stretched to the point where we feel like we will break and we cry out, "God, where are you?" It isn't until we come through the trial and look back and see the footprints of God, we realize we would not have survived what we just came through without His promised intervention.

Choosing Jesus has allowed me to walk in freedom in the midst of suffering. I believe with my entire being that God is always in control of my suffering. I can't say I always understand or even know the reasons for the trials I've had to endure, and the same is true for the trials I have yet to endure.

What I do know, with certainty, is that God always has and always will use my suffering for my good and for His glory.

If suffering is for my good and His glory, this means that the suffering will not be removed until God's perfect will is accomplished through it. He has proven more than faithful to sustain me when I am overwhelmed and completely consumed by my pain. It is when the duration of the trial seems to never end that I hold tight to the promise that says, "And the God of all grace, who called you to His eternal glory in Christ, after you have suffered a little while, will Himself restore you and make you strong, firm, and steadfast" (1 Peter 5:10). Our suffering has a beginning, and rest assured, ***it also has an end***.

I've referred to the "shadow of death" several times in this book. Immediately after Pat died, the shadow was always in front of me, leading the way. It set the course for my day. It dictated what I did and even how I felt because it was all I could see. Eventually, it was by my side. It was always in view through my peripheral vision, but it was no longer leading the way. I was learning how to laugh and enjoy life again but still felt an ominous gloom at various times. As my healing continued, the shadow took its place behind me. I know it is there, but it no longer demands all my attention.

I have "walked through the valley of the shadow of death" triumphantly with the One who walked through it before me.

Chapter 13
Finding Purpose in Suffering

Is suffering fair? I believe this is a legitimate question, and one I think everyone has asked at one time or another. The word *fair* is interchangeable with words such as *reasonable, just,* or *unbiased*. Based on the previous chapter, if suffering is deemed "unfair," then Jesus endured the worst unfairness of all.

Many of us have erroneously believed that if we live right, then we deserve a good life. In Ecclesiastes 7:14, however, we are told, "When times are good, be happy; but when times are bad consider, God has made the one as well as the other." We should expect that we are going to have difficult times in life. No one is exempt. For those who love to be in charge, it is a terrifying truth that we cannot predict nor control our future, so we find hope when we confidently believe that God is in control.

Jesus Himself foretold His suffering to His disciples, "He then began to teach them that the Son of Man must suffer many things and be rejected by the elders, the chief priests, and the teachers of the law, and that he must be killed and after three days rise again. He spoke plainly about this…" (Mark 8:31-32). He was not taken off-guard because He was expecting the trial before Him. That did not, however, keep Him from asking God to remove the grueling task of taking the sins of the world upon Him, but Jesus still resigned himself to do the Father's will.

Unlike Jesus, we rarely know the details of future trials, but even in this reality God says to us, "Dear friends, don't be surprised at the fiery trials you are going through, as if something strange were happening to you" (1 Peter 4:12 NLT). This particular verse was probably referring to the persecution the believers were facing, but I believe we can apply it to other forms of adversity in our lives. We need to be prepared to suffer knowing there is a purpose behind it.

Adversity definitely gets our attention. I read one time the following; "Small trials make us beside ourselves, but great trials bring us back to ourselves." Ben and Jenna were only twenty-one months apart in age. To say there were trying days in their toddler years is an understatement. On one particular day, they were impinging on my last nerve.

As I was heading for the kitchen with a dirty Sippy cup in my hand, I decided I could maybe relieve some tension if I threw the cup into the sink. I threw it all right, and with so much force that I broke the window above the sink. Two tiny blonde-haired children with eyes bugging out of their heads were quick to tell me, "Boy, are you going to be in trouble when Dad gets home." I failed miserably in handling this small trial.

It is the big stuff that makes us truly evaluate what is important and what place God has in our lives. The book of Job begins with Satan asking God, "Does Job fear God for nothing? Have you not put a hedge around him and his household and everything he has? You have blessed the work of his hands, so that his flocks and herds are spread throughout the land. But stretch out your hand and strike everything he has, and he will surely curse you to your face" (Job 1:9-11).

It was Pat's death that made me realize how tightly I wanted to hang onto things. He and I had a course set out for our lives. We had a beautiful home on Ten Mile Lake with our coveted treasures adorning each room. We had healthy, happy children whom we were so proud of, and we looked forward to experiencing together the unfolding of the plans God had for their lives.

We drove nice vehicles, took family vacations, and were part-owners of a business. In the midst of all these treasures, I had never bothered to ask myself, "Is my love for God dependent on the things He has blessed me with?"

St. Augustine said, "God wants to give us something, but cannot, because our hands are full and there is nowhere for Him to put it." Suffering empties our hands. Going through depression and demonic oppression emptied my hands of me. Up until that point, I was self-absorbed and independent. I received my identity from everything worldly. It was only after I released my grip and surrendered my identity in Him that I truly discovered who I was.

But in my tightly clenched fists, I was still holding onto the life that Pat and I had charted out before us. Would I blame God and turn my back on Him, or would I once again release my grip and see what God would place in my hands?

I've adapted the words from an unknown author that describes what I did.

> Once I held in my tightly clenched fist…ashes. Ashes from a burn inflicted on my forty-two-year old body. Ashes I didn't ask for. The scar was forced on me when my husband tragically died. I kept my fist closed, unwilling to release the dreams we had. Not even sure if I could. Black marks were left on everything I touched…so it seemed. The marks were always there to remind me that things would never be the same. I couldn't change my

> situation, but God could. His sweet Holy Spirit spoke to my heart one night in tearful desperation. He whispered, "I want to give you beauty for your ashes, the oil of joy for your mourning and the garment of praise for your spirit of heaviness." Beauty? Beauty for ashes? My sadly stained memories for the healing in His word? My soot like dreams for His songs in the night? My helpless and hurting emotions for His ever-constant peace?
>
> How could I be so stubborn as to refuse an offer such as this? So willingly, yet in slow motion, and yes, while sobbing, I opened my bent fingers and let the ashes drop to the ground. In silence, I heard the wind blow them away. I am now able to place my open hands gently around the fist of another hurting soul and say with confidence, "Let them go. There really is beauty beyond your comprehension. Go ahead—trust Him. His beauty for your ashes.

My previous trials had shaped me for ministering to others. Now, I can gently place my open hands around the hands of others who are hurting. God was asking me to comfort others with the same comfort I had received from Him.

"He comforts us in all our troubles so that we can comfort others. When they are troubled, we will be able to give them the same comfort God has given us. For the more we suffer for Christ, the more God will shower us with his comfort through Christ. Even when we are weighed down with troubles, it is for your comfort and salvation! For when we ourselves are comforted, we will certainly comfort you. Then you can patiently endure the same things we suffer. We are confident that as you share in our sufferings, you will also share in the comfort God gives us" (2 Corinthians 1:4-7 NLT).

My fiery ordeals made me far more sensitive to others who were hurting; a lesson I never learned in the classroom. I had to take the fieldtrip. To understand pain, I had to know pain, and only then could I reach out to others with compassion.

Before I could ever give comfort, I had to learn how to receive comfort. This was not always easy for me. My independent, self-sufficient nature tried to raise its ugly head again, and I needed to die to self in order to receive.

I learned an important lesson. When I allowed people to minister to our needs, it blessed them; if I had not allowed them to minister to us, I would have denied them that blessing. Our suffering not only drew us closer to God, it drew us closer to one another. First Corinthians 12:26 speaks of the body of Christ and says that if one part suffers, every part suffers with it. Family and friends suffered alongside us, and as we allowed them to meet our needs, it brought healing to their grieving souls as well.

To allow others to minister to me was actually a prerequisite to the developing ministry God was giving to me. As I let family and friends be the hands and feet of Jesus in my life, I was learning how to do the same in return. Being on the receiving end of another person's compassion taught me valuable lessons on what to do and what not to do when someone needs me.

The old cliché, "actions speak louder than words," is definitely appropriate in many instances. We have a tendency to want to fix things with our words; instead of stumbling over the right thing to say, just be there for the person. Meet their physical needs. Take care of small children. Run their errands. Clean their home. Treat them to a pedicure (a friend did this for me). The list is endless.

When people said to me, "I don't know what to say," I quickly gave them permission not to say anything. When they asked, "What can I do for you?" I let them know. I did not try to do it all on my own. I couldn't even if I tried. When in doubt, ask. The person you are ministering to is the only one who can honestly tell you what is needed.

The comfort and love I received from others encouraged me to live, and I wanted to help someone else choose to live when overwhelmed by the darkness. Pat's death was further transforming me into the person God wanted me to be.

In her Bible study entitled, *The Patriarchs,* Beth Moore shared in one of her video sessions that "our hardest tests involve our dearest loves. God is intentional in testing us to bring about results. Hard tests have huge effects, so when God is up to something hard, He is up to something big."[1] I don't believe that any crisis allowed by God is meant to destroy us. Rather, it reveals who we truly are.

I believe emotional pain, more than anything, is necessary for our growth in Jesus. I can't say that I've ever heard people testify they grew closer to God and stronger in character when their lives were free from pain and suffering.

The times I have grown the most in God were while on a journey through barren places—the hardest of the hard. Nothing could have felt more barren than when I lost my dearest love. But as I walked through this valley, I knew God more intimately when I got to the other side. I experienced His faithfulness more deeply. There was purpose in my suffering.

We all love mountaintop experiences; those extraordinary moments in life when we feel happy and excited about what we are doing and what is happening in our lives at that time. Times in the valley, however, are thought about with great dread and trepidation because they are linked to times of suffering. Have you ever been on top of a mountain? The view is spectacular, but there isn't a whole lot growing up there.

A valley, on the other hand, is beautiful. The vegetation is lush and often refreshing springs flow freely through the landscape. The elements are perfect for growth. There is a peace that beckons us to rest, but how easily that peace eludes us when we focus on the storm around us. But the peace is still there, and Jesus invites us to find it when He says, "Come to me all you who are weary and burdened and I will give you rest" (Matthew 11:28).

I have grown more in the tumultuous environment of the valley than anywhere else, and my growth has always led me to another mountaintop experience. And while I stand on that mountaintop, God instructs me to enjoy the beauty but to give special attention to the valley I just came through and see how beautiful He grew me while I walked its path of suffering.

God refines us in our time of suffering, and he lovingly explains why in Isaiah 48:10, "See, I have refined you, though not as silver; I have tested you in the furnace of affliction. For my own sake, for my own sake, I do this."

There truly is purpose in suffering. God uses adversity to purify us from sin and to strengthen our faith and commitment to Him as it forces us to depend on His matchless grace. God uses suffering to bind us with other believers, giving us sensitivity to their pain and allowing us to impart the wisdom we received in our times of trial. Suffering makes us long for God's truth, equipping us in discernment and in disciplining our thought life. Suffering stretches us in faith, hope, and character, making us grow into the men and women that God calls us to be.

After accomplishing such great things in our lives, we should be able to say with confidence, "My suffering has been worth it."

Chapter 14
Happily Ever After… Lives on Eternally

As I come to the last chapter of my book, I'm reminded that God has not yet written my life's final chapter. As long as He gives me breath in my lungs, my story will continue to unfold. I look to my future with undiminished hope and the assurance of knowing that I can walk through my final years in the freedom that Christ has purchased for me.

While my dad was living, he always said that people acted according to how they were dressed, which could ultimately have either a positive or a negative impact on their performance. As mayor of Fergus Falls, he always wore a suit and tie to council meetings. He saw this as a professional role, and he dressed professionally while performing in this elected office. His words have stuck with me throughout my life, and I've witnessed their truth not only in myself but also by observing others.

I have to confess that I still have many days when I do not like what I see as I look at the woman in the mirror. Menopause has set in, and the old gray mare, well, she "ain't what she used to be." I still have piles of clothes to put away before I can find my bed at night. On the days when I'm really discouraged by the image reflected back in the mirror, I know that it is time for me to meditate on God's Word, "The Lord does not look at the things people look at. People look at the outward appearance, but the Lord looks at the heart." (1 Samuel 16:7)

When it comes to clothing my physical body, the options I have are numerous—so many choices, yet so often a struggle. Each morning, however, God lays out for me a wardrobe of His choosing. It is the same every day, producing the same positive results of victorious living as long as I choose to put it on. It is my spiritual clothing that keeps my heart tender and fully His.

He has given me a beautiful belt, adorned with scriptural gems. He calls it "the belt of truth." It daily reminds me of the battles I lost when I did not have my belt securely in place, and instead, I listened to the lies of the enemy. As we have learned in *Mourning Journey,* Satan fights with lies and sometimes those lies can sound true. The best way I can detect a lie is by knowing the truth, so I tighten my belt each morning as I sit with my Bible in one hand and my cup of coffee in the other.

As the earlier verse stated, the Lord looks at the heart and Satan knows how valuable our heart is to God. I am not referring to the physical organ that beats but to the deepest part of our being where our emotions, self-worth, faith, and character reside. Satan loves to go after our heart. He tempts us to sin, hoping to lead our heart astray. When we have confessed sin, he still comes at us with accusations, introducing guilt and shame into our hearts.

But there, lying next to my belt, is a beautiful breastplate made up of God's righteousness. The words inscribed on it read, "God made him who had no sin to be sin for us, so that in Him we might become the righteousness of God" (2 Cor. 5:21). Every time I put on my breastplate, I'm remembering that an exchange has been made—my sin for Christ's righteousness. You would think a breastplate is cumbersome and restrictive. Not at all. My heart has never felt more protected than when I feel that plate next to my chest.

Living in Minnesota, much of the year is spent dealing with cooler temperatures. Even so, every morning, God has at the foot of my bed a pair of sandals…sandals of peace. He knows how much time I spent living apart from His peace in fear and anxiety. I broke his heart more than once when I pushed those sandals under my bed thinking they wouldn't keep me protected from the harsh elements, when in reality, they were exactly what I needed.

When I finally put them on, I realized that true peace only comes from knowing God is in control. I have nothing to either fear or be anxious about, and that peace I have spoken about that is beyond my comprehension daily fills my heart and mind as long as I walk in the shoes He has provided.

Thank goodness my purse has a strap to fit over my shoulder because I need a free hand to carry my shield of faith. Why in the world do I need a shield? Because I have fiery darts from the enemy being shot at me all day long in the form of discouragement, intimidation, low self-esteem, failure, and temptation, and this is only a partial list.

My shield of faith powerfully complements my belt of truth. When I see an arrow approaching, I hold up my shield and stand firm on the truth of God's word, and the flame is immediately extinguished. It is called the "shield of faith" because faith is an unshakable confidence. It does not only believe that God *can*, it knows without doubt that God *will do* what He has promised. Every day when I hold up my shield of faith, I'm saying, "The battle has been won."

I have never found a hat that I think looks good on me, so when God placed before me a helmet, I thought, "You have got to be kidding. Not only do I look ridiculous in a hat, it really does a number on my hair." God then says to me,

"Remember back, Lisa, to the times you feared you were losing your mind? Do you remember the harassing thoughts that bombarded you for years on end, spiraling you into times of depression? I'm giving you this helmet, the helmet of salvation, to protect you in your place of vulnerability, your mind."

Salvation means to be saved or delivered from. When I chose to follow Jesus, I was delivered from the works (accusations, temptations, and lies) of Satan. His power over my life had been broken, but he will continue to be relentless at going after my mind so that I won't believe he no longer has power over me. With the helmet securely on my head, I've never felt more protected.

With purse over my shoulder, shield in my left hand, my right hand is free to wield my sword, the final piece of my daily wardrobe. Everything I have put on up to this point has been clothing of protection. My sword, on the other hand, puts me on the offensive. It is the sword of the spirit representing the word of God. Reflecting off my sword is every other article I've put on, and it fills me with boldness.

At a moment's notice, I'm ready to thrust my sword into my enemy by proclaiming the word of truth, in faith. I'm guaranteed victory because of the assurance of my salvation, and the righteousness I have received fills me with peace. I am dressed for success. Thank you, Abba Father.

As faithful as God is to lay out my wardrobe each morning, I still have days and sometimes weeks where I step over the clothing He has provided in a hurry to dress my physical body. Not a wise plan. Failing to dress spiritually makes me prone to question if God really cares at all when I'm faced with times of testing. It is on my spiritually naked days that I find it easier to believe a lie than to believe the truth.

I have to admit, however, that I still have days when even though I'm dressed for battle, I'm so tired of the fight that I'm tempted to quit. It is on those days that I look at a stone placed on my kitchen counter with two dates written on it. The first is the date of Pat's death, and the second is the date Kevin and I were married. It is my stone reminding me of God's faithfulness and provision.

In Joshua chapter four, the Lord gave these instructions to the Israelites, "When the whole nation had finished crossing the Jordan, the Lord said to Joshua, 'Choose twelve men from among the people, one from each tribe, and tell them to take up twelve stones from the middle of the Jordan, from right where the priests are standing, and carry them over with you and put them down at the place where you stay tonight.'"

So Joshua called together the twelve men he had appointed from the Israelites, one from each tribe, and said to them, "Go over before the ark of the Lord your God into the middle of the Jordan. Each of you is to take up a stone on his shoulder, according to the number of the tribes of the Israelites, to serve as a sign among you. In the future, when your children ask you, 'What do these stones mean?' tell them that the flow of the Jordan was cut off before the ark of the covenant of the Lord. When it crossed the Jordan, the waters of the Jordan were cut off. These stones are to be a memorial to the people of Israel forever."

A memorial stone serves as a reminder to God's faithfulness in our past. When times get so difficult that you want to give up, a memorial stone is a sign to keep going, signifying that this, too shall pass, and you will be stronger because of it. The following story illustrates this effectively:

A man was sleeping at night in his cabin when suddenly his room filled with light and the Savior appeared. The Lord told the man he had work for him to do and showed him a large rock in front of his cabin. The Lord explained that the man was to push against the rock with all his might.

This the man did, day after day. For many years, he toiled from sun up to sun down, his shoulders set squarely against the cold, massive surface of the unmoving rock, pushing with all his might. Each night, the man returned to his cabin sore and worn out, feeling that his whole day had been spent in vain.

Seeing that the man was showing signs of discouragement, Satan decided to enter the picture by placing thoughts into the man's mind such as: "You have been pushing against that rock for a long time, and it hasn't budged. Why kill yourself over this? You are never going to move it."

Thus, giving the man the impression that the task was impossible and that he was a failure, these thoughts discouraged and disheartened the man even more. "Why kill myself over this?" he thought. "I'll just put in my time, giving just the minimum effort, and that will be good enough."

And that he planned to do until one day he decided to make it a matter of prayer and take his troubled thoughts to the Lord. "Lord," he said, "I have labored long and hard in your service, putting all my strength to do that which you have asked. Yet, after all this time, I have not even

> budged that rock by half a millimeter. What is wrong? Why am I failing?"
>
> To this the Lord responded compassionately, "My friend, when I asked you to serve me and you accepted, I told you that your task was to push against the rock with all your strength, which you have done. Never once did I mention to you that I expected you to move it. Your task was to push. And now you come to me, with your strength spent, thinking that you have failed. But, is that really so?
>
> "Look at yourself. Your arms are strong and muscled, your back sinewed and brown, your hands are callused from constant pressure, and your legs have become massive and hard. Through opposition, you have grown much, and your abilities now surpass that which you used to have. Yet you haven't moved the rock. But your calling was to be obedient and to push and to exercise your faith and trust in My wisdom. This you have done.
>
> "I, my friend, will now move the rock." (Author Unknown)

The stone in my kitchen is a visual reminder of God's provision for me. Even though there are only two dates recorded, it represents His faithfulness throughout my life. More times than I care to remember, I felt like I needed answers to my struggles before I could move on. But God gently reminded me that knowing Him was enough. Jesus was and forever will be the cornerstone I press into. I become strong in Him, He moves the rock, and I am better for it. "I can do all things through Christ who gives me strength" (Philippians 4:13).

My stone of remembrance has also served as a reminder of God's faithfulness as I speak testimony of what He has done for me whenever I'm asked, "What does this stone mean?" What it signifies to me the most is, "He who began a good work in me will be faithful to complete it" (Philippians 1:6).

There is a poem that was written by an unnamed Confederate soldier. It typifies the life of so many of us, asking God to give us the riches of this world, thinking that is our happily ever after. Listen to where he discovered life's truest blessings:

I asked God for strength, that I might achieve;
I was made weak, that I might learn humbly to obey.
I asked for health, that I might do greater things;
I was given infirmity, that I might do better things.
I asked for riches, that I might be happy;
I was given poverty, that I might be wise.
I asked for power, that I might have the praise of men;
I was given weakness, that I might feel the need of God.
I asked for all things, that I might enjoy life;
I was given life, that I might enjoy all things.
I got nothing I asked for; but everything I had hoped for.
Almost despite myself, my unspoken prayers were answered.
I am, among all men, most richly blessed.

I had asked for "happily ever after" and then mistakenly believed it had died with Pat. Happily ever after is an eternal concept. From the moment Christ became my Savior, I have possessed eternal life, and that is my happily ever after.

So in reality, it never died.
It has been and forever will be mine.

Epilogue

A decade has passed since we said our earthly good-byes to Pat Schultz. It would have been easy to get stuck in anger and bitterness over the things he has missed. Benjamin married his beautiful Celeste in a ceremony on the shore of Ten Mile Lake. They have two amazing children, Nathalie and Noah, with twins on the way. Twins! Just like Papa Pat and Uncle Mike.

Jenna married her prince charming, Matthew. She often says how much he reminds her of her dad. I'm not surprised she is drawn to a man with his same qualities. They also have two amazing children, Lincoln and Kaelyn. Both grandsons were named after their papa. Pat's full legal name was John Patrick, and now we have Lincoln Patrick and Noah John. I know that brought a smile to his face in heaven.

Jared, too, is now married. How he treasures his precious Rachel. They do not have children yet but are enjoying life together in Boston, Massachuesettes while Jared finishes grad school.

At each wedding, we felt Pat's absence, and tears of sadness were mingled with our tears of joy. Each grandbaby has been a reminder to all of us that life goes on, and we look for Pat in their eyes, their smiles, the shape of their hands, and their personalities. Though they will never meet Papa Pat, they will know him through the endless stories we will share.

I feel incredibly blessed in life. Kevin is an amazing husband who graciously welcomes Pat's memory without feeling threatened by it. He is Papa Kevin to the grandchildren, and they are crazy about him. He truly loves my children and their spouses as if they were his own, and he shares in their pain when they are missing their father.

The children and I have not gotten stuck in bitterness and anger over Pat's death because we have chosen to live in the abundance of God's goodness in the midst of what seems unfair. Living in despair would not honor Pat's life nor would it carry on his legacy.

As you read the tributes of the children to their dad, you will discover that they truly have learned what it means to "suffer strong." I'm so honored to be their mom.

Hey Dad, I can't believe that it has already been over ten years since you've been gone. It seems like only yesterday we were getting up to go duck hunting or taking our yearly trip out to Mott, ND for our week of pheasant hunting. I am so thankful for that time that we got to spend together, just the two of us and the things that you taught me about work, family, and loving the Lord.

In many ways, I feel like I am following right in your footsteps and have the same hopes and dreams that you had when you were my age. I remember when I was younger and going to school, I couldn't wait for class to be over so that I could get off the bus and go run to look for you on the resort so that I could help in some way. We both loved the resort so much, and I am glad that I have been able to follow in your footsteps to continue to work at the resort. When I am there, it makes me feel closer to you in a way that is hard to explain, but it gives me a peace to know that we both have poured blood and sweat into our family business.

As I sit here now writing to you, my kids are running around the house playing. Noah keeps running around yelling," Dadda! Dadda!" and it puts a big smile on my face to hear him. It's amazing how much more respect I have for you now that I have my own children. People say, "Just wait till you have your own children." It is so true. My life has truly changed since we have these two beautiful children, and I give you a lot of credit in helping me raise them.

I thank you much for the values you instilled in me and the life lessons I learned from you—how to work hard, to take care of my family, to help those in need, and most importantly, to love the Lord. I still miss you a lot and will forever, but I am thankful for the years that we did have together because those were the most important years of my life. I love you and miss you!

Benjamin

***

From the moment my dad first laid his eyes on me, I was forever his little girl. And he was forever my hero. I never imagined that I would only get to spend a short seventeen years with him before he went to live with our heavenly Father. There was never a day that I questioned his love for me. I will never forget his laugh and joking side. I will never forget how he taught me to ride a bike and how we played sports in the yard. I will never forget our father-daughter dates. I will never forget sledding down the hill by our house or skating on the lake. I will never forget our summers on the resort. The memories are endless, and the time I had with him I will treasure forever.

There aren't a lot of women who have to decide who will walk them down the aisle. It's an automatic that their fathers will. I did not have that option. I'm so thankful for the close bond between my family and that my brothers were willing to step up to the plate. Each brother, one on each side, took my arms and led me down the aisle. As tears streamed down my face, I thought of my dad and how proud he would've been to be a part of that special day. Psalm 30:11-12 says, "You turned my wailing into dancing; you removed my sackcloth and clothed me with joy, that my heart may sing to you and not be silent. O Lord my God, I will give you thanks forever."

I wish my dad could've experienced life as a grandfather. I wish he could've been there after the birth of my children. To see the way he would've looked at them, the same way he used to look at me. That look that they are loved more than anything else in the world. Even though my children will never meet my dad on this earth, they will know all about him. I will cherish sharing all of my memories with them. And they will know how much he would've loved them.

1 Peter 5:6 -7 says, "Humble yourselves, therefore, under God's mighty hand, that he may lift you up in due time. Cast all your anxiety on him because he cares for you." Our life on earth is so short compared to eternity in heaven. I'm thankful that I will get to see my dad again. And so I say, "See you soon, Dad. I love you forever."

Jenna

***

Dad,

It's been over ten years since I last saw you. Not a day goes by that I don't think about you or the day you passed. I am so blessed to have had you for a father. You set an example for our family of how to live a life of integrity and what it means to use the gifts God gives to further His kingdom. There have been so many difficult days since you've passed. I have felt sad, frustrated, and angry countless times since you died. Sad when you haven't been at holidays or major family events. Frustrated seeing my friends who still have their dads taking them for granted. Angry that you were taken when I was so young and that you missed out on so much of my life. The hardest part, though is not having the opportunity to have gotten to know you better. One of my biggest regrets is that I was too young for us to become really good friends. I was still maturing in my life when you passed, so when you died, I not only lost my dad but also lost the chance of having a really good friend.

As sad and as angry as I have been at God for missing out on these opportunities I could have had with you, I know that He has used your life and death to further His kingdom, and that makes it all okay. It was evident in the weeks and months after your death that God was using your life and death to glorify Himself. Because of you and the life you lived, a countless number of people were able to hear about God and see what it looks like to serve Him. You may not have known it, but so many people were impacted by the way you served God through the way you lived your life.

I wouldn't be where I am in my life if it wasn't for you. You showed me in your life what it means to live for God. You showed what it looks like to give selflessly of your gifts to help and to serve others. You were a man of integrity, the same man each and every day that people could trust and lean on. I hope and pray that one day I can be a man that lives life the way you did.

I hope that I would make you proud. I love and miss you so much. I'm looking forward to the time that we will see each other again.

Jared

***

When Pat died at such a young age, I remember people saying, "What a waste. He was so young with so much life ahead of him." It was statements such as these that brought me back to the verse I shared with you in the first chapter when Mary anointed Jesus with the oil. The disciples were indignant at Mary's actions and asked, "Why this waste?" The perfume was worth a year of wages. Even the expensive flask that contained the perfume was broken in order for it to be spilled out, making her act even more costly.

Jesus rebuked the disciples and came to the defense of Mary, praising her for her loving act of devotion. You see, nothing given to Jesus in love is ever wasted. I had to come to the place of giving Pat over to Jesus, knowing that his death was not a waste because God, to this very day, continues to use his death to speak life into others through the story He has given me to tell. If just one person is changed or encouraged, then his death was not a waste, and God's promise to me has been fulfilled that one day He would use me to help others be free.

As we read in the Bible's account, in order to anoint Jesus, Mary had to pour out the perfume. In that one act, she was pouring out her love and devotion to Christ. And in one timeless act, God poured out His love to us when He sacrificially gave His One and only Son to die on a cross for you and me as payment for our sins.

It is sin that separates us from God, and on the cross Jesus was willing to take our sins upon Himself. Isaiah 53 says it best, "But He was pierced for our transgressions, He was crushed for our iniquities; the punishment that brought us peace was upon him and by his wounds we are healed." Jesus, broken and spilled out for us.

You might be asking, "What must I do to be saved?" The Bible says that when we confess with our mouths and believe in our hearts that Jesus is Lord, we will be saved. It is as simple as saying, "Lord Jesus, I am a sinner in need of your saving. I ask you to forgive me of my sins, and I invite you to be the Lord of my life. In Jesus's name, Amen."

If you prayed this prayer, I want to be the first to say, "Welcome to your happily ever after."

Notes

Chapter 2: Innocense Lost

1. https://www.nlm.nih.gov/medlineplus/ency/article/003213.htm.

Chapter 4: Who is the Woman in the Mirror?

1. Dictionary.com.
2. http://jokes-post.com/Three-Ladies-in-a-Sauna/0_212_best=-1_menu=-_object=38651_order=date.aspx.
3. The Bondage Breaker, Copyright © 1990, 1993 by Harvest House Publishers Eugene Oregon 97402.

Chapter 5: My Journey to Freedom

1. The Steps to Freedom in Christ Copyright 1990, 2001, 2004 Neil T. Anderson
2. Adapted from The Steps to Freedom in Christ

Chapter 6: The Labor Room of Sorrow

1. Dictionary.com

Chapter 7: Grieving with Hope

1. The Patriarchs, Published by Lifeway Press © 2005, Beth Moore

Chapter 8: Living a New Normal

1. Life Application Bible copyright © 1988, 1989, 1990, 1991 by Tyndale House Publishers, Inc., Wheaton IL 60189. All rights reserved.
2. Ibid.

Chapter 12: Why I Chose Jesus

1. http://www.charismamag.com/blogs/fire-in-my-bones/17198-how-jesus-endured-the-pain-of-the-cross
2. The McArthur Study Bible, © 1997, Word Publishing

Chapter 13: Finding a Purpose in Suffering

1. The Patriarchs, Published by Lifeway Press © 2005, Beth Moore

Acknowledgements

I wish to personally thank the following people. Without their contributions and support, this book would not have been written:

To my chosen children, Celeste, Matthew, and Rachel: You were first loved by my children and chosen by them to be their life partner and because of their choice, my life is immeasurably blessed. Please know that I love you like my very own. Thank you for believing in me.

To my Dad (at home in heaven) and Mom: Thank you for the love you shared that gave me life. Thank you for always having faith in me, which often gave me the confidence to do the seemingly impossible…like writing a book!

To my precious sisters, Linnae and Lori: You are two of the most selfless and giving women I know. Thank you for loving your baby sister and for always having my back.

To my in-laws, Jerry (at home in heaven) and Shirley Schultz: Thank you for giving birth to a son who became one of my most coveted treasures. I'm so sorry for your loss and so grateful for your love. The entire Schultz family is my forever family. I will be eternally grateful for their support and encouragement during the writing of this book.

To my brother-in-law Mike and sisters-in-law Sue and Lisa: Thank you for putting down on paper your tribute to your beloved brother and for allowing me to share your words with my readers.

To my in-laws James (at home in heaven) and Darlene Fred: Thank you for giving birth to a son who knows and practices selfless love of which I'm the recipient. I adore him. I am beyond grateful for your prayer covering over our lives. Thank you Darlene, for the many prayers you prayed over me as I wrote this book.

To Dr. Neil Anderson: There is no word in the English vocabulary to express my gratitude for the ministry of Freedom In Christ. When I was introduced to this ministry, I knew Jesus as my Savior but I did not know Him as my liberator. The truth has set me free! Thank you Neil for writing the foreword to my book and for all of your insights during my writing journey.

To Kirsten Danielson and Olivia Hoffman: Thank you for the beautiful front cover. You captured the picture in my heart and brought it to life.

To Al & Debbie Carlson: Thank you for the sanctuary of your home as a place for me to write. Thank you, Debbie, for all the conversations we had about my book and the insights you gave me that helped clarify my message. I wish I could adequately put in words how much I appreciate you.

To Jim Koenig, Jacqi Glen, Olivia Hoffman, and Kirsten Danielson: Thank you for proofreading my completed manuscript and giving my book the finishing touches it needed. I appreciate you reading **Mourning Journey** *with a critical eye in the midst of your busy lives.*

To Deana Riddle: Thank you for the professional look you gave to my book in the design of its cover.

To Rik Hall: Thank you for formatting my book, giving it the professional look I desired it to have.

To my editor Madalyn Stone: We have never met face to face and yet I feel I know you. You looked at my words and in your edits you kept my voice so that it never quit being my story. Thank you for helping my dream to write a book come true.

To Steve Harrison and the Quantum Leap Coaches: There were many days I was in tears and wanting to close my computer and forget that I ever started writing a book. My investment in Quantum Leap kept me motivated and kept me from quitting. Thank you coaches for pushing me to be the best I could be. I've feasted at your buffet and my heart is full.

Meet the Author

Lisa Schultz-Fred is an author, speaker and Bible teacher. She is also a Ministry Associate and a Trained Encourager with Freedom In Christ Ministries. For decades, Lisa has been presenting life-changing messages to help women know their identity in Christ and how to walk in freedom even in the face of life's darkest moments. She has been educated as both a speaker and author through Bill and Steve Harrison's Quantum Leap Coaching Program and through Proverbs 31 Ministries. Lisa makes her home in Minnesota with her husband Kevin.

If you would like to contact Lisa for a speaking engagement or follow her ministry, please visit her website at:
www.lisaschultzfred.com or contact her at
sacredpresspublishing@gmail.com.